(From left to right) Louisa, Herbert and Emily Pepys.
From the pastel by Catherine Esther Gray, 1843.

THE JOURNAL OF
EMILY PEPYS

with an Introduction by

GILLIAN AVERY

PROSPECT BOOKS

Acknowledgements

The publishers would like to thank Dee Cooper most warmly for the idea of publishing the Journal, for making the text available and for writing the account of its discovery. They are also grateful to Mary Winnington-Ingram for further information about the Pepys family and for showing the originals of the portraits; to Derek Pepys-Whiteley, former Keeper of the Pepys Library at Magdalene College, Cambridge, for scholarly advice on the family tree and his note on the pronunciation of the name Pepys; to R. E. Alton for suggesting the cover illustration; to Ken Brooks for providing the engravings and drawing the map and family tree; and to many friends who gave encouragement by their interest and enthusiasm.

Cover illustration: Detail from 'The governess' by Richard Redgrave, reproduced by courtesy of the Victoria and Albert Museum, London.

First published in England in 1984

Printed and bound in Great Britain by
SMITH SETTLE
Ilkley Road, Otley
West Yorkshire

Contents

Preface by Dee Cooper   *page 5*

Introduction by Gillian Avery   *page 9*

Family portraits
Louisa, Herbert and Emily Pepys   *frontispiece*
Maria Pepys, Emily's mother   *page 22*
Henry Pepys, Bishop of Worcester, Emily's father   *page 23*

Family tree
The Pepys family   *page 21*

Map
Emily Pepys' country   *page 25*

Facsimile
Page of the Journal for 20th July 1844   *page 26*

The Journal
4th July 1844 to 26th January 1845   *page 27*

Preface

I was fourteen when I first discovered Emily's journal. For as long as I could remember the little book with the worn covers had stood among the Jeffrey Farnols and Rider Haggards on my grandmother's bookshelves, but to my childish eyes it had looked too uninteresting to bother with. Then one wet afternoon I was looking for something to read, and I took it out.

It was very fragile and had lost one or two pages. On the fly leaves a smudged, childish copper-plate stated: 'Arthur Nutt is a good boy. A good boy is happy', over and over again. Arthur Nutt was my grandmother's uncle. Other pages, left blank by Emily, had been used as a diary and shopping list, written in a hand which I recognised as that of my grandmother's Aunt Polly Nutt, herself an enthusiastic diarist. The date of Aunt Polly's first entry showed that the diary had been in my grandmother's family since at least 1870.

Emily's journal was written in a firm, neat hand which, in spite of blots and crossings-out, seemed far too mature for the ten-year-old she proclaimed herself to be. I sat down that first afternoon and read it from cover to cover. The vitality and directness of her style immediately brought her to life for me, not just as a typically Victorian child, full of anxiety to improve her character and do good in the world, but as a surprisingly modern miss, delighting in games and pranks, in gossip and in gently malicious comments about her friends and neighbours. I found Emily enchanting.

My grandmother could shed no light on the diary's history or on how it had come into my family's possession. She confirmed that it had been given to her by her maternal aunt, but had no idea of its previous history. The name Pepys meant nothing to her. No-one else in the family seemed at all interested in the diary, so my grandmother gave it to me.

For several years the diary remained among my books; occasionally I re-read it and wondered about its origins, but I was busy studying and it was not until I was working in an architect's office that Emily took her next breath of fresh air. I was talking one day to a young architect whose father was a keen local historian who had traced his own family back to the seventeenth century. I mentioned the diary and the mystery of its origins and he suggested that we should do a little detective work to find out who Emily was and what relation, if any, she was to me.

We had plenty of clues to follow up. We knew her name and date of birth, the names of her brothers and sisters, cousins and friends. Judging by the ease with which the family visited Worcester, Stourport and Kidderminster, the geographical location of her home should not be hard to work out. Her father obviously had clerical connections — Emily speaks of him going to consecrate a church — and the family appeared to have considerable social standing, since her parents were invited to dine with the Queen Dowager at Witley Court. We tried Debrett's Peerage. It didn't take long to discover that Emily was the daughter of Henry Pepys, then Bishop of Worcester, whose official seat was Hartlebury Castle, near Kidderminster.

We decided to make a pilgrimage to Hartlebury, which at that time was untenanted, as the see was vacant. The curator, Mr. Munday, was very helpful. He showed us the library where Emily and her brother had helped to arrange their father's books, the schoolroom, scene of the Christmas Day fire; the great stone hall, a portrait of Emily's father still on the wall, with at one end the double doors through which the Stourport fire engine must have been driven to get to the moat behind the castle. Outside we found the avenue where the children practised their archery and the gardens where they had worked so hard to carry out the improvements planned by 'dear Mama'. Now we are able to visualise so many of the incidents described in the diary in their proper setting, the people too seemed to come to life again and walk with us through the house and grounds. It was a moving experience.

Mr. Munday was able to give us more details of the Pepys family. Emily herself fulfilled her ambition and married a clergyman: Henry Lyttleton, younger son of Lord Lyttleton of Hagley Hall, Rector of Hagley and Hon. Canon of Worcester. She had spent her married life at Hagley rectory and there we followed her, to a delightful house, set in the grounds of Hagley Hall with its own small church nearby. In the churchyard we found a simple stone: Emily Lyttleton. Born 9 August 1833. Died 12 September 1877. Poor Emily; she died, childless, at the age of 44.

On that visit to Hartlebury we were told of a great-nephew of Emily's, a grandson of her sister Louisa, who was Archdeacon of Hereford. Some months later we visited Archdeacon Winnington-Ingram, who very kindly gave us all the information he could about the family and promised to circulate a transcript of the diary amongst any members who might know anything more of Emily. He had a further valuable contribution to make to the search for Emily: a set of four delightful watercolour portraits of the family painted only the year before the diary was written.

The puzzle of how Emily's journal found its way onto my grandmother's bookshelves is still unresolved. Perhaps one of my ancestresses was the 'Nana' mentioned by Emily, and took the journal with her as a memento of her young charges when she was finally replaced by the dreaded French governess. Certainly my family were all living in that part of Worcestershire in the 19th century, but other than that there seems to be no connection. It is significant that Aunt Polly Nutt was already using up the blank spaces in the journal six years before Emily's death.

One thing more must be mentioned: within a year of our visit to Hartlebury I was married to the young architect who had helped so enthusiastically with the search. I think Emily would have been pleased with what she would certainly have called 'a little piece of matchmaking'.

DEE COOPER

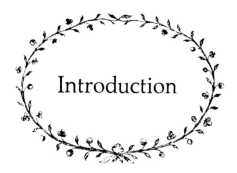

Introduction

All the charm and life of this diary is concentrated in a brief six months. So what we are shown is Emily as an impish yet earnest child, forever ten years old, her boon companion Herbert, a fourteen-year-old schoolboy, Louisa poised on the edge of the adult world, Henry a remote under-graduate — none of them ever to grow up. It is an early Victorian tableau vivant, the Pepys family, their friends and relations momentarily assembled for us, and then the curtain falls again, and we can only con-jecture what became of them all, and try to piece it together from family genealogies that survive.

Ten years old is a good age to begin a diary. You have a reasonable ability with words, and you are not yet afflicted with the tedious self-consciousness and literary aspirations of adolescence. Of course, some young Victorians were made to keep diaries by Authority, with self-improvement (both literary and moral) as an aim. Marjory Fleming (a pre-Victorian writing in 1811) managed not to be blighted by the adult supervision imposed on her. 'It was the very same Devil that tempted Job that tempted me I am sure but he resisted satan though he had boils and many other misfortunes which I have escaped. I am now going to tell you about the horrible and wretched plaege that my multiplication gives me you cant conceive it — the most Devilish thing is 8 times 8 and 7 times 7 it is what nature itselfe cant endure . . '. But Marjory is unique; diaries that are written for adult approval are normally stilted and hopelessly prosy.

Emily's diary is for herself; she records in it things that she would not 'tell anyone else for worlds'. She is three years older than Marjory, therefore the way she writes is less remarkable. On the other hand those extra years have given her the stamina to persist and provide us with the continuous narrative that Marjory's small, weary hand had not the energy to set down. Nor could Marjory, aged seven, observe personalities so knowingly. Here are a family's jokes, quarrels, hopes and disappointments — all the matters that are usually forgotten by the time the mature adult comes to write memoirs. The awfulness of the Christmas Day fire would be remembered, perhaps, but not the tedium of a dull sermon, the blissful sense of release when the music master's cold forces him to cancel a lesson, the exquisite funniness of seeing 'no end of things' above Lady Foster's knees. The diary is proof of how many rainy days there are (and how much they afflict one) in summers that an adult recalls only as long and hot. Would middle-aged Emily ever admit, even to herself, how she and Herbert, in the absence of their elders 'looked at several nice things in the Encyclopoedia, such as Anatomy Midwifery etc. etc. etc. but Mama told me to go to bed 10 minutes before 9 so we had not much time. Herbert and I always together let one another into all our secrets that we would not tell anybody else for worlds'. Odd how a child's conscience works: Emily is scrupulous to obey the orders about bedtime when her mother is away, but has no hesitation in reading what she must have known would be forbidden. The Pepys were an easy-going family by early Victorian standards, but articles on anatomy and midwifery, one can feel tolerably certain, would come on the Index. After all, Emily herself knew that Mama would forbid certain books when the box came from the circulating library. (She chose *Pickwick*, because that was safe; probably Louisa was around to keep an officious eye on her little sister.)

The impression we form from Emily's diary is of a conscientious but unspiritual, well-connected family, fully aware of how they stand in society and aware of how others stand too; after all, when Emily remarks of the Bishop of Hereford 'and he is only a tailor's son' she must be repeating what she has heard her elders say. They are certainly not High Church, nor do they manifest any evangelical fervour; they are comfortable, middle of the road, sensible, moderate, in no way given to excess, believing that the world is a very good place for those who conduct themselves properly, that nothing in it need be altered.

And this impression is borne out by such details of Bishop Pepys' career that survive. He was the third son of Sir William Pepys, the first baronet, and descended from the John Pepys of Cottenham (died 1589) from whom Samuel Pepys was also descended; Samuel was the great-great-grandson; Henry three generations further removed. It should be stated at this point that only Samuel's branch of the family called themselves 'Peeps'; the other members of it have invariably pronounced it 'Peppis'. (See Note.)

Sir William (Emily's grandfather) seems to have been a gentle and delightful man with strong literary inclinations who consorted with the *bas bleus* of the 18th century, and whose life and letters were published in 1904 in two volumes under the title of *A Later Pepys*. Of his three eldest sons William succeeded to the baronetcy and died unmarried; Charles (obviously the most able) rose to be Lord Chancellor and was created Earl of Cottenham, and Henry, Emily's father, after his education at Harrow and Cambridge, went into the Church. He was a Fellow of St. John's College, Cambridge, for 17 years, but from a letter written to his patron the Earl of Hardwicke in 1812 we learn that he was keen to get away from Cambridge: 'I feel somewhat distressed at the prospect of remaining for life a Fellow of a College, or of being at last turned out to grass upon a College living, not kicking up my heels and snuffling the breeze, like Homer's horse, but with broken spirits and relaxed energies dragging on the evening of life in my solitary pasture.' The request which followed for help in obtaining the appointment of Chaplain to the Speaker failed, but in 1818 he was appointed . . . Rector of Aspenden, Hertfordshire, holding with it the College living of Moreton, Essex. It was while he was Rector of Aspenden that he married, in 1824, Maria Sullivan, daughter of the Right Honourable John Sullivan.

In 1826 he was appointed a prebendary of Wells, and in 1827 rector of Westmill, Hertfordshire, where Emily was born, and which she refers to, remembering Joey Yorke from those days (Joey was a grandson of the Earl of Hardwicke; his father, the Rev. and Hon. Grantham Yorke, later became Dean of Worcester). Of Henry's parishes in those days his father wrote, presumably without a vestige of irony, that the young man had 'two good livings, in one of which he placed a very good curate, and as it

[11]

was within easy reach, he could occasionally attend to its concerns'. Very much the attitude that we find in *Mansfield Park*, where Sir Thomas Bertram commends Edmund's conscientiousness in actually taking up residence at his living. Emily says that she would like to marry either a clergyman or a gentleman of independent means. Clearly the two are almost the same breed to her mind, as they would have been to the Bertrams.

In January 1840 Henry was elevated to the bishopric of Sodor and Man, was installed in May and left a year later, almost to the day, on his translation to the see of Worcester. So when Emily's diary begins they have been at Hartlebury Castle for four years, and at Hartlebury the family stayed until the Bishop's death in 1860. 'We were talking today of Papa's being made Archbishop of Canterbury,' says Emily, adding that that is the only thing she would like if he were to leave Worcester, though she would not object if it was Winchester. 'Papa says he would not refuse London if offered to him.'

But it never was. The nearest he got to translation was in 1848, when his name was put forward with two others as possible successors to Howley at Canterbury. That he got as far as this seems to have been because Lord John Russell had his choice considerably narrowed by the fact of fourteen of the bishops having opposed him in one of those ecclesiastical *causes célèbres* that rocked the Victorian church — the Hampden trouble. Dr. Hampden was a divine about whose orthodoxy there was some doubt, whom Russell proposed to present to the see of Hereford, which had become vacant at about the same time as Canterbury. Bishop Phillpotts talked openly of Russell going about like Diogenes with his lantern to find a dishonest man who would consent to become Archbishop of Canterbury for the express purpose of consecrating an unworthy man to a bishopric. Henry Pepys in many ways would have suited the Prime Minister, a well-connected Whig with, one suspects, an Erastian outlook. In the event it was Sumner who succeeded Howley, and Pepys was one of the three Whig bishops who assisted at the consecration of Dr. Hampden a month later.

He was, the *Dictionary of National Biography* assures us, very popular in Worcester, and conscientious in the discharge of his diocesan duties.

Of these duties we are given fleeting glimpses by Emily, who often talks of Papa going off on some social jaunt with Mama to stay in country houses, and less frequently of his consecrating 'some church or other'. (Never, curiously, of a confirmation, though these were rarer, and larger, occasions in dioceses where railways communications were poor.) She records Papa preaching sometimes in their own parish church at Hartlebury, though his sermons do not stir her, she prefers the Rector's. One of these occasions is 'Sacrament Sunday', a reminder of how infrequently communion was administered in those days. The habit of weekly communion was growing in the forties and fifties, but rural areas were slower to take up the practice, and as late as 1864 there were plenty of parishes that celebrated the Sacrament only four times a year.

As a bishop he would have had to attend the House of Lords, and Emily's diary begins as they leave their London house in Grosvenor Place, and ends as they are about to set off for it again. Henry Pepys, it seems, spoke no more than twice in the Lords, and then only on ecclesiastical matters of small importance, though he voted, as might be predicted, in favour of all the chief liberal measures. His published writings are scanty, six charges to the clergy of his diocese, two single sermons, and a memoir of the son of his patron, Lord Hardwicke. In sum, one might say, rather a secular bishop, who in these days would probably not have entered the Church at all. He feels nostalgia for the good old days before the established church act of 1836, when the stipends of bishops had been equalized so that, to quote an extreme example, Durham could net £19,066 while Llandaff had to be content with £924. By the time Henry Pepys went to Worcester the stipend had been levelled down to £5,000. 'Papa says that if he had his whole income, i.e., what the other Bishops used to have, he would go to the seaside at this time of the year, as he says it is so unwholesome when the leaves are coming off.' (However, Emily could content herself by reflecting that the Bishop of Hereford, in the neighbouring diocese, received only £4,200 — a fact she no doubt was fully aware of, worldly little madam.)

The Pepys family at the time of Emily's diary consisted of (beside Bishop Henry and his wife Maria) Henry, born 1824 (he later became registrar of the London Court of Bankruptcy), Louisa, born 1827 (who

[13]

was to marry the Rev. Edward Winnington-Ingram), Herbert, born 1830, who went into church and held the living of Hallow in Worcestershire, and Emily, born 1833. Two children had died in infancy, and there had also been two more daughters, Albinia and Georgiana, between Louisa and Emily, who had died, as Emily mentions sorrowfully, of scarlet fever, probably not so very long before the diary opens, since Herbert finds his gold pencil case in 'poor dear Binny's desk' which apparently has not yet been sorted out.

Other members of the Pepys family come on visits, or are visited. Charlotte and Emy, for instance, who are mentioned in the first entry, are cousins, considerably older than herself, daughters of her father's second brother Lord Cottenham. Charlotte (1822 − 91) became one of those intrepid Victorian lady travellers, and was to write books about her experiences in Russia. Emily meets them at Tandridge in Surrey, which was the home of her father's eldest brother, Sir William Pepys (he is buried at Tandridge). The Sullivans and the Tylers who are greeted with such affection when they come to Hartlebury are also cousins, on her mother's side. Maria Pepys' maiden name was Sullivan, and her sister Harriet was married to Captain George Tyler R.N. The Tylers' home was Cottrell, Glamorgan, but difficult of access since the Worcester to Cardiff line had not yet been built. We note that one of the Tylers, Gwinnet, has followed his father into the navy.

We never meet Emily's beloved, Teddy, nor does he even bother to write to her. This is what one would expect from an eleven-year-old boy; it is Emily's crush on him that seems unusual in the pre-adolescent stage. But though she is faithful to Teddy during the six months of the diary, she concedes that the flame does not burn so very high. The only time she has *really* lost her heart is to 'Villiers Lister, a very handsome boy about 11 years old, with long curls . . . yet the actual love only lasted 1 night'. (If that particular love had lasted longer Emily's subsequent life would have been rather different, as the handsome boy became Assistant Under Secretary of State at the Foreign Office and Deputy Lieutenant of Radnorshire.) In fact Emily's attitude to Teddy is so severely practical that we guess she has been imitating her elder siblings and only taken on a beau because it seems no young person ought to be without one. 'If I do not see Teddy soon I shall give him up, as there is no use loving a boy one is never to see.'

Whether her schemes for getting Teddy to the nearby school (could it have been Bromsgrove?) ever came to anything is not known. But Teddy did go into the Church, as she has so fervently wished (even though she didn't marry him) and became Vicar of Portbury, near Bristol. Other cousins are mentioned, the Whateleys, for instance, children of Henry Pepys' sister Maria, and at Pull Court, near Upton-on-Severn, which they visit fairly frequently, lived Edmund Dowdeswell, Emily's great-uncle.

We hear a lot about the Bakers. The Rev. Thomas Baker is Rector of Hartlebury (a very lucrative living this, worth £2,188), and the Rev. Henry Niven (little Snivens, as they refer to him contemptuously) is his curate, who is eking out his income by taking in pupils. Herbert is one of them, and Mama seems to share her children's disdain and to take a certain amount of pleasure in telling the poor man that she intends to send Herbert, who is being prepared for Cambridge, somewhere else when he is sixteen. Mr. Niven must have been a man of some scholarship, as he was a Cambridge Wrangler, and is admitted to have musical tastes. But he obviously has not the right connections to smooth his path in the church, and furthermore he is small and ungainly and a figure of fun.

The Peels, who live in great style and give dances (indeed Emily reckons that they spoil their children with the good things of life), are also a clerical family. John Peel, brother of the Prime Minister, was at that time Vicar of Stone, near Kidderminster, though he does not reside in the parish but at Waresley, near Hartlebury. Peel became Dean of Worcester in 1845. At the time of the diary he was also a prebendary of Canterbury, and had to spend a certain amount of time in residence there, as Emily remarks. She is probably thinking of them when she wishes that Papa too could give a ball—but he can't as he's a bishop. There is certainly a good deal of dancing at Hartlebury Castle, but probably not on the scale that Emily would wish.

The Disbrowes are mentioned as close friends. They were not land-owning gentry as were the rest of the Pepys circle (where they were not clerics). Edward Disbrowe was knighted in 1831, and as there is mention of the family going to live at The Hague, he may well have been in the Diplomatic Service. Henry Pepys junior was later to marry — not Jane Disbrowe, mentioned as an early love, but Louisa, her sister.

One's immediate impression of the Pepys family is — in spite of all the housefuls of visitors — of close-knit domesticity. The girls have been taught by their mother (though there is the dreaded possibility of a French governess for Emily); even Herbert is not sent away to school. The Bishop's own father was devoted to his family, spent much time with his children (whom he educated himself when young), and Henry Pepys obviously inherited this ability to make a happy home. It well may be this close relationship that accounts for Emily's mature outlook; we notice that she hardly thinks of herself as a child; 'we ladies' she says on one occasion, and remarks of a visitor, who is in fact her own age, that she seems like a child and they have nothing in common. So Emily sits up to dinner parties, goes to all the local dances. The only difference between her and Louisa seems to be that when Louisa comes out she is able to go to the public balls.

Still, Emily is a child and the childishness does sometimes break through in Daisy Ashford-style pronouncements. She is not old enough, for instance, to detect irony, or to see through heavy adult humour. When Mr. Talbot says '"Have you made any conquests in London?" I blushed deeply and faintly said "no" for I thought of Villiers Lister . . . Mrs. Talbot looked very *glum* [She well might at her husband's crude facetiousness] as if she was a wee bit jealous, though I am sure she need not fear, for I do not care for Mr. Talbot, on the contrary I think he takes great liberties, and is sometimes very tiresome to me.' The circle obviously spends a great deal of time in discussing who loves who, and match-making, conversations from which Emily is not excluded, and which she somewhat prematurely applies to herself. No doubt Teddy Tyler, if he had known the full extent of her plans for him, would have been deeply alarmed.

Of the taboos and proprieties which so saturate the novels of Charlotte Yonge — we remember for instance the elaborate rules about chaperonage, the scandalized horror when thirteen-year-old Gertrude May takes off shoes and stockings on the sea-shore — a code that is often taken as representative of the attitudes of all early Victorian society, we find little trace. True, Mama is firm about the polka, she 'does not like us to dance it with gentlemen except brothers and cousins', and Emily 'of course' does not dance waltzes. Perhaps this is only allowed when she comes out, there is no suggestion that they are wrong for her elders. Charlotte Yonge deprecates both dances in her earlier novels, and the more conservative of her families would not have allowed them at their balls, confining themselves to country dances and quadrilles, though even with her the polka by the 1860's seems established and safe, and by the 1880's she goes so far as to permit waltzing at a Girls' Friendly Society party. It is interesting to note that Emily's elders seem to get opportunities for flirting, and that Harriet Sullivan (Emily's own age) goes round hugging and kissing her cousins, even Herbert. Charlotte Yonge had said, remembering her own childhood in the 1830's, that even girl cousins were not allowed to embrace each other. Only one other thing, beyond the polking, is Mama shown to be firm about: handkerchiefs. She does not approve of lace ones and 'she does not like us to carry handkerchiefs, as she thinks it is nasty'. Precisely the view of my own mother if, without pockets, I tried to carry my handkerchief in my hand.

What sort of person was Emily? How would she have grown up? It is difficult to forecast at ten (or eleven, as she became in the course of that six months); she is going to change so much. We can say that she is gregarious, sociable, practical, affectionate, conscientious, but not of a very religious turn of mind, admitting honestly that she does more things for the praise of Mama than for the love of God, and that she does always 'dislike going to church and is always glad to get off it if I can'.

Her attitude to the less fortunate is what we would expect of her class and time. 'I do so like going among poor people if they are clean and do not cry as some do,' she remarks as she accompanies her parents to a cottage to present some baby clothes. 'Her present baby is too old, I should think, but it will do for the next one, if they have another.' (We get here one of the few glimpses there are in the diary of life outside upper class Pepys circles. The cottage consists of two rooms, and there are six children living at home.) This sort of distribution of soup and flannel to the deserving poor would go out of fashion as the century moved on. Even during the time of Emily's diary Mrs. Pepys' heart doesn't really seem to be in it: she can't even be bothered to get to the cottage before the baby grows out of the clothes. She takes rather more interest in the village school which, as doyenne of Hartlebury, she supervises with the Rector's wife.

There are touching glimpses of Emily striving to improve herself. When the diary opens she has just been given *Influence* to read and is busy trying to absorb its lessons. This rambling moral tale belongs to a previous generation. Published in 1822 by A Lady (in fact, Charlotte Anley), it follows the strivings and backslidings of Ellen who, though well-principled, is easily influenced and wavers between the heady joys of high society and the sober 'methodistical' ways of the Welsh vicarage where her earliest and best friend lives. Eventually society wins, and the upright (and wealthy) young man who has been contemplating her as a future wife is disgusted and goes back to his native Switzerland. Ellen then gives herself up to a religious life, falls into a decline and dies. The book is prefaced in the manner of the time with elaborate apologies by the author for having written a novel at all since many parents 'would very properly exclude all romances from the libraries of their children'. It is a reminder of how different in this respect Emily's childhood is from her mother's. Her mother tells her that there were few children's books in her day; she did not even know *The Child's Own Book*, Emily says with amazement. Though one cannot of course be certain, this is likely to have been the collection of tales which originally appeared in 1830 under the joint imprint of Alfred Miller (London), Henry Constable (Edinburgh) and Milliken (Dublin). It was very popular and went through many editions, and was later taken over by Tegg. Containing French fairy stories and tales from the *Arabian Nights*, as well as retellings of Gulliver's adventures in Lilliput and such English stories as Goody Two Shoes, Philip Quarll and the History of Little Jack, it was a most unusual publication for its time — when there was strong moral disapproval and suspicion of fairy stories and indeed all works of imagination for the young. Although by Emily's time these were making a return, they would certainly have been under an interdict in Maria Pepys' childhood.

But Emily does not really seem to be a bookworm. She talks about

[18]

books occasionally, but not with the air of one to whom they matter a very great deal. Mention is made of *Martin Chuzzlewit*, which had come out in parts between 1843 and 1844, and to *Pickwick*, which by this time was almost a classic (it had appeared between 1836 and 1837). Papa reads *Pickwick* to them, an indication of how popular Dickens was as a family writer. (Charlotte Yonge however was one of those who disapproved of him, considering him a coarsening influence.)

Christmas was celebrated far less lavishly in the 1840's. Of course that particular Christmas of 1844 was marred by the fire, but probably there would have been no presents anyway; these were to come on New Year's Day, when all the children had a gift from Mama. Indeed the only piece of Christmas revelry mentioned is the decoration of the schoolroom with mistletoe and holly which they painfully shape into 'Jolly Christmas'. 'I thought of "Christmas" and Herbert thought of putting "Jolly" before it.' (True, the servants did have a dance, off-stage.)

The details of medical treatment show how little could be done in those days. Albinia and Georgina had died of scarlet fever, so did poor Mrs. Wood. It was only the resilience of a patient that could carry him through illness, the remedies available being positively destructive. William Buchan's *Domestic Medicine* for instance, a very popular work originally published in 1783, which went through many editions until well into the next century, and which was much used in the ordinary home, prescribed purges and blood-letting for every disorder. Emily gets many 'a nice dose of jalop' (purgative) whatever her complaint, whether it is toothache or a cold, and Mama purges herself even more drastically with calomel and 'a black dose' in an attempt to get to grips with her lumbago. She gets better; people mostly do if they have faith in the remedy.

On November 14th Papa and Mama go to stay at Hagley Hall, in Worcestershire but not within easy driving distance. Hagley was then the home of Lord Lyttelton (and is now that of Viscount and Viscountess Cobham, who have opened it to the public as a 'stately home'). Ten years later Emily married his brother, the Rev. and Hon. William Henry Lyttelton, born in 1820 and therefore thirteen years older than herself. At the time of the diary he was still a curate but he was soon to take over the family living at Hagley. Emily died in 1877, and three years later her husband married again, Constance Yorke, daughter of the Grantham Yorke mentioned in the diary, and sister of Joey and Edith and Alice. In this year he became Canon of Gloucester.

It is an unjust world; there is William Lyttelton surrounded with the good things of the world, the family living at an early age and a snug canonry to shelter him in his later years. And there is Mr. Niven — little Snivens — a Wrangler (William Lyttelton only scraped a third in the Cambridge Classical Tripos) having to be content, after a curacy of ten years, with the tiny parish of Bishampton, near Pershore, and an income, Crockford tells us, of £140, about a quarter of what his former pupil Herbert was getting in his own Worcestershire parish. Inevitably one is reminded of the Rev. Josiah Crawley, the perpetual curate of Hogglestock and all those unpaid butcher's bills. (*His* stipend was £130.) It would be pleasant to think that preferment came Mr. Niven's way. But in 1889 he is still at Bishampton, still with the same income. In 1890 Crockford no longer carries his name.

Emily, however, had fulfilled her ambition: she married a clergyman, who was probably also a gentleman of independent means. No doubt she was able to help the poor of Hagley and oversee the school there, and perhaps gratify her love of dancing and good company at Hagley Hall. And certainly during the early years of her marriage, until her father's death, she was living close enough to her beloved family to be constantly in touch with them. There seems to have been only one cloud in her sky. 'I have made this description in case I get married and have children it may be useful to them,' she writes in an account of a normal morning of lessons. Alas, there were no children to enjoy her description or to inherit their mother's talents.

GILLIAN AVERY

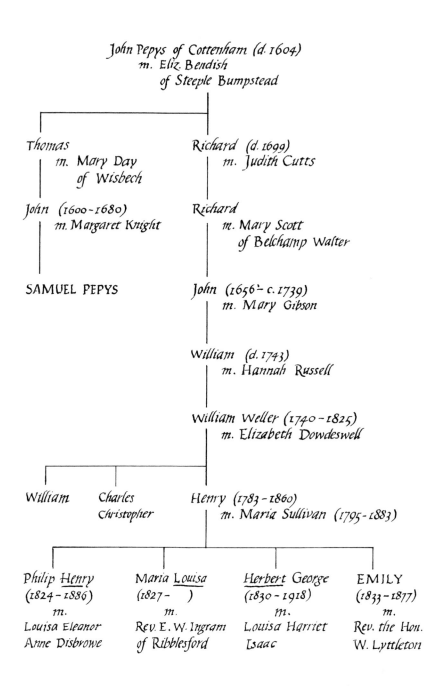

The Pepys family

Maria Pepys, Emily's mother

Henry Pepys, Bishop of Worcester, Emily's father

Note on the pronunciation of the name Pepys

The Pepys Cockerell branch of the family, descendants of Samuel Pepys' sister, still pronounce their surname 'Peeps Cockerell'; and in Cambridge, where in Magdalene College the Pepys Library contains the manuscript in shorthand of Samuel's diary, the pronunciation 'Peeps' is invariable.

I believe the two-syllable pronunciation 'Peppis' may have been generally adopted comparatively late, say not earlier than the mid-18th century, and adopted partly on the ground that one of the earliest of the many different spellings was 'Pepiz', and partly perhaps because unmarried lady members of the family objected to being called 'Miss Peeps'!

Robert Latham, editor of the definitive edition of Pepys' Diary (1972) (Vol. VI, p.173) states: "There is little room for doubt that [Samuel] pronounced his name 'Peeps'", and gives cogent reasons for this view. There is equally no doubt that Emily and all in her wide family circle pronounced their surname in two syllables 'Peppis'.

DEREK PEPYS-WHITELEY

Note on spelling and punctuation

Emily's original spelling and punctuation has been retained in the printed version of her Journal. Words and phrases which she underlined (sometimes twice!) have been set in italic.

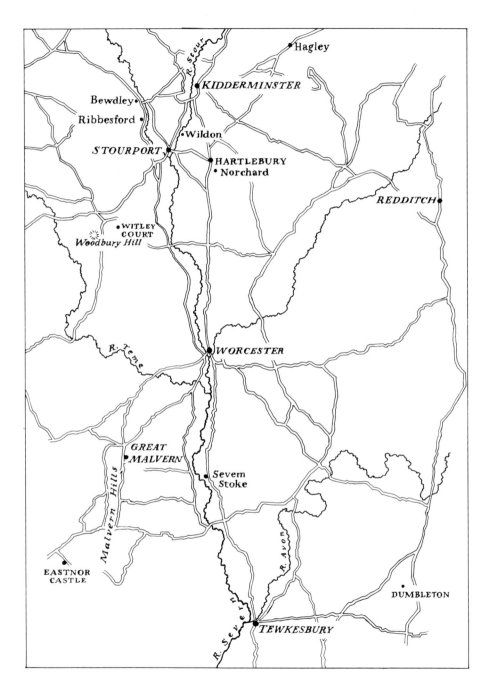

Emily Pepys' country

at Louisa & Herbert, not knowing the least
what he meant till at last he said "Did
you win any body's heart in London" I
blushed deeply & faintly said "no" for I
thought of Villiers Lister, though that did
not amount to "winning his heart" I believe,
Mrs Talbot looked very glum & if she
was a wee bit jealous, though I am sure
she need not fear, for I do not care for Mr.
Talbot, on the contrary I think he takes
great liberties, & sometimes is very tiresome
to me. Louisa & I played our Duet, & the
first thing Mama said this morning was
"How execrably bad you played your played
your Duet last night" but I did not think
so. We went to bed about 1/2 p.t. 10.— Sunday 21st —
Up & dressed by 1/4 p.t. 8 this morning to breakfast,
as Mama, Papa, & the company went to
Worcester to see the Judges go to the Cathedral.
We went to Church, & had a sermon from
Mr Baker, which was rather too old for me,
so I did not pay much attention, & the Church

Page of the Journal for 20th July, 1844

Journal
belonging to Miss Emily Pepys
who began to write it
July 4th 1844 aged 10
her first Journal.

July
1844

Thursday, July 4th, 1844. Tandridge. Arrived here from Grosvenor Place about 5. Found Charlotte and Emy Pepys here and liked them both very much, Charlotte particularly, as she was very good-natured to me — Emy having asked me for a lock of my hair, I asked Mama to cut a bit, which she did, though it was very small — Emy says when she has money, after having covered the chairs in the breakfast-room which are very dirty, she will make a brooch with my hair.

Sunday, 7th July. Went to Church in the morning and had a very dull sermon which I do not think I learnt much from, as I am afraid I did not pay much attention.

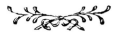

Monday, 8th July. Botleys. Arrived here about 6 — was very sorry to leave Charlotte and Emy and did not expect much fun here . . .

[A page of the Journal is missing here.]

[27]

. . . with 4 horses, though as it rained very hard, I was not allowed to go on the box. On our arrival we found the four twin lambs put out before the house, with all their coloured ribbons round their necks.

Sunday, 14th July. Went to our own dear church, but we should have liked to have heard Mr. Baker, though Papa preached a very nice sermon, so did Mr. Niven in the afternoon. A beautiful day, and we went out in the evening and talked of Henry's early loves — Miss Osborn — Chaddy Taylor — Jane Disbrowe and I think that was all.

Monday, 15th July. A beautiful day. In the afternoon Mama and I went to the school, which I always like very much. I think in that way I shall be quite fit to be Teddy's wife, as he is going to be a clergyman. I long to go to Mrs. Clark's to give her my baby clothes. At Botleys they gave me a book called "Influence" to read, and I think it did me a great deal of good, the "Ellen" there was so like me, and I only hope I shall improve as she did. Since I read that I have felt much happier, and have prayed to God much oftener than I used. Last night at Desert Papa and Mama told me to go to bed at 9 instead of half past which I am sorry to say I did not do as I ought to have done. Instead of saying "Hey me" and gone when I was told, I began speaking crossly, and said that Mama told me I need not go till half past in the summer, but I hope another time I shall be a better girl. In reading "Influence" I had a good lesson how nothing can be done without praying to God to help you, so I have prayed that I might do what I was told without being cross. Mama told me yesterday that Alfred Tyler would not come here certainly and most likely Gwinnet would not, therefore I thought of course, [. . .]   and Teddy would come or at least some of them, but when I asked Mama, she said that she was not very anxious to see them, whether she has guessed about Teddy and me I do not know, but I hope he will come at all events.

Thursday, 18th July. I am happy to say Mama has written to Aunt Harriet to ask her to bring her two girls and to leave the *three* boys in charge of their tutor, which though of course I am very sorry Teddy does not come yet it is something to have Cay and Louy. Aunt Harriet has not answered the letter yet, so we do not even know whether they will come but I hope they will. Mama also wrote to Mrs. Stuart Sullivan to ask her and Harriet and Katey to come here for a few days which of course I shall like very much, though Herbert does say that they are two romping bouncing girls. I am very fond indeed of Harriet from the little I saw of her in London. Being so nearly my age and so exactly like me in every way, I certainly think we shall be great friends: I hope she will love me! I think Katey will get rather in the way, but I shall see when the time comes. Perhaps Herbert may take a fancy to her and get in love with her, but then I am afraid he will get in my way, though I ought not to think so. Their answer is not come yet, and I dare say never will come, as we do not know exactly where they are. If the Railroad is made from Worcester to Cardiff how jolly we shall go to Cottrell. Teddy has not written to me for a very long time, but I have written to him very often.

Friday, 19th July. A very showery day, and a little thunder. The Bishop of Durham and Mrs. Maltby, Mr. and Mrs. Sandford came here yesterday to stay till Monday. I like the Bishop very much and all the rest tolerably; the Bishop is very deaf with one ear, which is rather disagreeable. Today we went out in the morning but being caught by a shower of rain we were obliged to come in and then I did not go out again as I was obliged to come in to do my horrid music which I think is a great bore sometimes. This afternoon we went to Stourport to see about a boat which Papa is going to let us have; the man showed us one which Papa said was too long and narrow, and I think myself it was not a very safe one. He says it must be 20 ft. long and 5 ft. broad, but the man said he would be about a month making that, and as we want it by the time the Tylers come here, that would not exactly do, so I think the best way will be, either to write a note to the man at Bristol and ask him to send us one as we know the size, or else to ask Gwinnet to go down to Bristol and get us one, but I hope we shall get one soon anyhow. Last night Louisa and Herbert played at

Chess, I read "Martin Chuzzlewit" and the others talked. After tea I went to bed, and even offered myself, which I thought at the time was very good, but was no more than I ought to have done. Tonight Herbert and I had a conversation about being shy. I think Mama says that being shy is merely being afraid of what people think of you. Tonight we had a dinner party, Mr. and Mrs. Ingram dined here, and Mr. and Mrs. Claughton dined and sleep one night. At Desert I sat next to Mrs. Claughton which I liked very much, as I like her very much; we talked and even laughed a great deal, and it was altogether very pleasant. After Desert we were idle part of the time and then for something to do we went to the round table to look at some medals and to say "Yes, that is very *Bewe-we-we-weteful*" which was not very amusing, even so dull that Herbert went to bed. A little time after that Mama at the request of Mrs. Claughton, played the Polka. A little time after that Henry and Louisa at the request of the same person, began to Polk, and then I was very sorry that Herbert had gone to bed as I had nobody to Polk with. Mrs. Claughton and Mama sang a Duet and then Mrs. Claughton sent me all the way to the Pink room to get her singing book, which I was very glad of, as I like obliging anybody I like. After that Mrs. Sandford sent me all the way to the Blue Room, or rather to the end of the Gallery, to get her Music Book, but when I had got there Mr. Sandford came running out, and said he thought he could get it quicker than me, "a great insult to such legs as mine". About 11 went to bed.

Saturday, 20th July. Was up and dressed at 8 and instead of doing lessons went out with Louisa and Mrs. Sandford and was very tired. When I came in to my great delight I found Mama had had a letter from Mrs. Stuart Sullivan to say she would have great pleasure in coming here with Harriet and Katey on Saturday next to stay till Wednesday. After breakfast we went out and Mrs. Claughton insulted me (as she generally does once every time she comes) by saying, when I offered her my hand down the steep steps, "Much good you would do me if I was to lean on your hand" which I did not like at all. After luncheon Mama and the company went out in the carriage — Henry and Herbert went out riding — and

Louisa and I went in the park to read. I read the "White Lady" a *ghost story*, then we talked about the delightful time to come when the Stuart Sullivans come and then the Tylers and the Disbrowes, then we came home. We had another dinner party tonight, Mr. and Mrs. Talbot, Mr. Hastings and Captain Winnington. At Desert I took my glass to Papa and asked for a little wine, and while I was there Mr. Talbot said to me "Young Ladies generally ask their partners how they are". At first I did not know what he meant, as I did not remember having danced with him, but at last I remembered having danced with him at Mrs. Peel's. It was very awkward for me as I could not go up and put my hand between him and Mrs. Maltby to shake hands with him. After Desert we were sitting together and all of a sudden he came up to me and said "Have you made any conquests in London". I looked at Louisa and Herbert, not knowing the least what he meant till at last he said "Did you win anybody's heart in London". I blushed deeply and faintly said "no" for I thought of Villiers Lister, though that did not amount to "winning his heart" I believe. Mrs. Talbot looked very *glum* as if she was a wee bit jealous, though I am sure she need not fear, for I do not care for Mr. Talbot, on the contrary I think he takes great liberties, and sometimes is very tiresome to me. Louisa and I played our Duet, and the first thing Mama said this morning was "How execrably bad you played your Duet last night" but *I* did not think so. We went to bed about half past ten.

Sunday, 21st July. Up and dressed by quarter past 8 this morning to breakfast, as Mama, Papa and the company went to Worcester to see the Judges go to the Cathedral. We went to Church, and had a sermon from Mr. Baker, which was rather too old for us, so I did not pay much attention, and the Church was dreadfully hot. The Text was from 17th John Gospel 8th verse, it was a charity sermon for the Christian Knowledge Society. Mama gave us each half a crown apiece to put in. In the afternoon we had a dull sleepy sermon from Mr. Niven—thought of Teddy and Harriet S. Sullivan all the time. Mama came home about 6 dreadfully tired. Judge Tindal, Marshall Tindal and Marshall Erskine dined here today. Marshall Erskine took Louisa into dinner and I thought seemed

[31]

rather "tender towards her", but perhaps it was only a small piece of flirting. He seemed a nice young man, and I don't think I should object to having him for my brother-in-law. It was a very warm evening and we went out for a little while.

Monday, 22nd July. All the company went away, even Papa; he went to Birmingham and comes back Saturday next. A very awfully hot day, and we went to call on Mrs. Baker and were nearly baked.

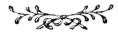

Tuesday, 23rd July. Another very hot day and now I am nearly roasted.

Wednesday, 24th July. Herbert and I have proposed to make another harmonicon as now we have only three instruments and four to play. I am going to make one for Louisa. We have great fun now in the morning when we go out in having small concerts out of doors. This morning we sat down in the boat and played. This afternoon I have not been quite so good as I ought to have been, as when Mama told me to do my work I did not do it at first as it was so dreadfully hot, but after a long time I did 6 stitches. When Mr. Sandford was here, he said he would get us some bows and arrows in London and we expected them last night but they did not come. At present we propose shooting by the side of the avenue which will be a very nice place I think. I hope soon we shall be good *Archers and Archeresses.* I think at least our bows and arrows will come tomorrow. This evening we went out, but it was very damp and foggy, and altogether I did not like it at all and I almost thought something was going to happen.

Thursday, 25th July. I had the oddest dream last night that I ever dreamt; even the remembrance of it is very extraordinary. There was a very nice pretty young *lady,* who I (a girl) was going *to be married to!* (the very idea!). I loved her and even now love her very much. It was quite a settled thing and we were to be married very soon. All of a sudden I thought of Teddy and asked Mama several times if I might be let off and after a little time I woke. I remember it all perfectly. A very foggy morning but Henry said it would be fine, but I do not think it has. It feels very *thundery*. This afternoon we began making our Harmonicons. I did not succeed very well, and got rather out of patience. Sent one piece to the Carpenter to plane, as that is the only thing we cannot master. Went out for about half an hour. It rained hard, this evening, so we did not go out.

Friday, 26th July. Not a very fine morning, we went out on the common. A beautiful afternoon, I and Mama went to the school, and then about the garden and I believe she means to alter it. Rather cold and damp in the evening, so I did not go out, and Louisa went out and came in again . . .

[A page of the Journal is missing here.]

. . . in till 9 which they got a great scolding for as Mrs. Sullivan said they were told to come in 20 minutes before. Talked of Uncle John's children. All agree that Minnie is the "proudest little ape" they ever saw. They like the others I believe. Harriet is a great deal too fond of kissing — every minute she is hugging and kissing. Herbert says he likes her very much, only she hugs him so which is rather "improper". She cried in the park today, and when I asked her why after a long time she said I had been so cross and disagreeable to her, but I am sure it was only in fun if it was at all. I do not like Katy, she is so very cross and ill-tempered though she does not look as if she could be. Nothing goes on all day but "Do not be so very disagreeable".

Tuesday, 30th July. Did not like either very much this morning, as they would do what they were asked not. They spoilt my Harmonicon and

[33]

when I mended it, they would not leave off, so I was obliged to hide it. Liked them better in the afternoon, settled to write to each other. Showery day.

Wednesday, 31st July. This is the sad day on which I and the dear Sullivans are to part. Harriet gave me a dear little Seal, she gave Louisa a purse and Katey gave Herbert a little Memorandum book. I remember saying to Harriet, what fun it would be if Katey and Herbert were to get in love though I do not think there is much chance on Herbert's side. Katey cried when she went away, but I think Harriet was most sorry to go. I mean if I can to send her a little present when I write to her. A very wet day.

August
1844

Thursday, 1st August. Another wet day. Papa had a letter from the boat-builder at London to say he had got a boat already made for either £42 or £22 which remains to be settled. This afternoon Mr. Murrey (the Bishop of Rochester's son) came, he is rather a nice man and shy. We went out on the common. Felt very lonely as the Sullivans are gone. Saturday we are going in to Worcester and must get something for Harriet if I can but I have not the least idea what to get as I have only got 3/8d. to get anything with, but I dare say she will be satisfied with nearly anything.

Friday, 2nd August. Today Papa went to consecrate a Church near the Giant's Grave, near Kidderminster, a very pretty spot, and Mama and Mr. Murrey went with him. Was rather fidgetty about Papa and Mama as they did not come home till much later than they expected. A cold wet day.

Saturday, 3rd August. A very wet day, so we none of us went to Worcester except Papa, so I was not able to get anything for Harriet. Today everybody is cross to me except dear Mama and Papa who never are. Henry is unbearing. It is all I can do to restrain my temper, which I am afraid does break out rather oftener than it ought to do. Sometimes I cannot help crying. Our bows and arrows came last night though now it

[35]

is so wet that we cannot shoot. I think Mr. Sandford must have forgot them till Papa wrote. We began shooting yesterday and liked it very much. I shoot at present about 40 yds. I should think. Sometimes I shot very bad and sometimes pretty well but never hit the target. Louisa hit it twice, once in the red and once in the outer white but then she shot much longer than we did as she shot before breakfast and after dinner. Of course Henry shot the best as he is used to it at Cambridge but he did not hit the bull's eye once. I was not so much laughed at by Henry as I expected but he seemed to think my shooting a horrid bore. As I only shoot about half way I have my turn after the others have all done, which I do not like so much. I have hit the target twice but just as I expected Henry said there was not near so much merit in my hitting it as I only stood half way.

Wednesday, 7th August. This being Mama's birthday we had a holiday and were out shooting all morning. Louisa did not hit the target at all for some time but at last she hit the *bull's eye* which I shall for the future call the *gold* as that is the proper name. Have got a cold in my head. I was determined to be the first to wish dearest Mama "Many happy returns of the day" on her birthday, so of course was glad of an excuse which was, that I was to go in at about 7 and ask if I might go out. At the same time I wished her the "happy returns". I wanted to give her her present at breakfast time as we always do, but Louisa, Henry and Herbert all said that we had better not, as the Stuarts were in the house. Our present was a box-wood case for letters answered and unanswered—Papa's was handsome velvet workbox ornamented with gold. Altogether she seemed to like her presents very much. Last Monday the Charles Stuarts came and I like them both very much. They stay till Saturday. I forgot to say Mrs. Wood had a little son last Sunday and when Papa came home from Worcester he said they were both doing well, but the Stuarts went there today and they said she was very ill: she had got the Scarlet Fever, that horrible disease that took off my two dear sisters Albinia and Georgy, and which I am afraid will take off poor dear Mrs. Wood. I am very sorry both for her and for Mr. Ingram, but I hope she will get better.

Thursday, 8th August. This evening the Tylers came. Gwinnet came but only till Monday. They came about 10 o'clock very cold and hungry. Gwinnet set down to some cold lamb and ale with a pretty good appetite considering he had been on a steamer; though he is a midshipman he did not like the steamboat at all: he seemed to be just the same as he used to be, and just as fond of Nana (alias Gormans). I do not think any of them are the least altered. We went to bed very soon. This was Nana's birthday; we gave her a pair of ear-rings which were 16 shillings. Mama paid 10 as it was a great deal for us to give. In the evening Tiny (alias Maria) said "The boys send their love Emy, and hope you will write soon.", though it is their turn over and over again. I should very much like to have a little private letter from Teddy to show me his heart, and also I should like to see him again to revive my love.

Friday, 9th August. This is my birthday, I am eleven years old today. Henry Louisa and Herbert gave me the prettiest little penholder I ever saw. It was white spotted with something bright—a little ring of Turquoises round the bottom—a little silver hand to hold the pen, with a ruby on its finger. Mama gave me a nice little Harmonicon, it was not quite such a nice one as the first one I had, which is now spoilt, but it has very good tones. Of course we had a holiday.

Saturday, 10th August. Today the Stuarts went away, and also Miss Millish and Miss Smith did, who I believe I forgot to say came on Thursday. It was tonight too that we heard of poor dear Mrs. Wood's death: she was quite delirious poor thing, but was sensible before she died. She asked to see her baby and the doctor said she should see it the next morning. "I do not think I shall see anybody tomorrow morning" was her answer, meaning she would be dead, but she did not die till 11 o'clock the next morning. She was a dear creature, and though she was so much older than me I was as fond of her as anybody; she was about twenty I think, and had just had her first child, who is, I believe, at present quite well, though it did go and see its poor mother before she died. I am afraid she must have caught from the doctor, who was attending her in her confinement. It is indeed a sad thing for the poor parents, but all we can say is "God's will be done". He alone can support us in the hours of trial. I believe poor Mr. Ingram was heard to utter a piercing shriek when the news of her death was brought to him. Since we have been here that family has had nothing but misfortunes, a son first, then a son-in-law, then a nephew and lastly poor Mrs. Wood who they doted upon. Tonight Tiny fainted at dinner time, what from I do not know: she said she did not feel well and went upstairs. As soon as she was gone Aunt Harriet said Toddy and Louisa had better go and see after her; no sooner had they got to the top of the stone stairs than she fell, fainting, into Louisa's arms (I should think she was rather heavy). Toddy took her as soon as she could, and Louisa went to call someone. James (the footman) was the first to come and carried her to her own room, then of course mother sister cousins and maids went to her and she soon recovered.

Sunday, 11th August. Not a very fine day. Went to Church both morning and afternoon. Had a beautiful sermon in the morning from Mr. Baker, who seemed to preach it upon Mrs. Wood's death, as it was upon that subject. It was the first sermon I ever heard that I was sorry when it was over, but I really was in this, for I felt that probably as soon as I was out of the church I should forget it. I do not think I ever heard a more affecting sermon. In the afternoon it rained as we went and we came back. Had a dull sleepy sermon from Mr. Niven, not to be compared to Mr. Baker's.

Monday, 12th August. This is the day Gwinnet was to have gone, but he has got leave till tomorrow; the servants packed all his clothes up thinking he was going this morning. Today the Fosters came, who I do not care much about. I really do not know which I like best, Toddy or Tiny (alias Harriet and Maria) but I rather think Tiny. We *polked* this evening and danced the Lancers. I think I forgot to say in its right place, of Robert Peel's dancing the Polka, on my birthday. He did it in the most ridiculous manner, just as they would dance it in the Opera, with his arms akimbo, and all sorts of figures, and dreadfully out of time. Louisa was the first to dance with him.

Tuesday, 13th August. Today poor Gwinnet went away at half past five, so that we were obliged to wish him Goodbye over night. Of course we felt lonely without him, and I do not think we shall see him again for a long time. In the afternoon, Papa Tiny Louisa and I went out walking. The conversation turned upon what profession her brothers were to be in. I am very sorry she said dear Teddy wanted to go out to India, which I should not like at all, as I should like to be a clergyman's wife. When we were at Cottrell he said he was to be a clergyman, and when I go back I must try and persuade so to be. We polked again this evening.

Wednesday, 14th August. A very rainy morning: Tiny and I played at Battledore and Shuttlecock, as we could not go out, we kept up to 175, which was pretty well for me. Toddy and Henry played at Coronella, and kept up between 20 and 30. I copied "La valse a deux tempes" for Mama, as Toddy has been teaching me to write music, I did not do it very well though. In the afternoon Aunt Harriet and I went to Mrs. Peel's but did not find her at home. After that Tiny and I took a little walk in the garden and I liked her very much.

Thursday, 15th August. This is the day poor dear Mrs. Wood is to be buried. Louisa saw the hearse returning when she was out riding. I think she ought to have been buried sooner, as the Scarlet Fever is so very infectious. Poor Mr. Wood has caught it. This evening the Disbrowes came, Sir E. Disbrowe, Lady Disbrowe, Charlotte, Jane Teddy and Willy. Charlotte is 22, Jane is 16, Teddy is 10 and Willy is nearly 9. Jane drank tea with us this evening, as she had not time to dress for dinner. She showed me a trick, viz. Take a piece about 4 inches long, and tie it together, then twist your fingers in it, put your two thumbs and two fingers together taking hold of the string all the while, then manage to separate your two

[39]

thumbs from your two fingers, and let the string slip through, but you must shut them again directly, so as to make people think you slip it through without separating them. The boys are very rude at tea-time and at breakfast.

Friday, 16th August. Went out in the morning with Jane and in the afternoon too — a pretty fine day.

Saturday, 17th August. In the afternoon we took a drive to Ribbesford and home by Bewdly. Mrs. Ingram is very well and Mr. Wood is better.

Monday, 19th August. Today we all went to Woodbury Hill in a carriage and fly, and riders, 15 of us. We had some capital fun, and came home quite safe, and I liked Jane very much. I think I forgot to put down, what capital fun we had getting over the stiles, with Lady A. Foster. She could not manage it a bit, and got over so slow, and pulled up her petticoats so high, that there was no end to the things we saw above her knee. Jane and I did laugh so about it, I thought we never should recover. I love Jane.

Wednesday, 21st August. Today there was a grand cricket match at Waresley against the Stourport Club, we all went to see it, but I am sorry to say the Stourport beat, by a hundred. Herbert Peel plays very well, and was very much applauded. I am rather laughed at about Herbert Peel, as Robert happened to say that when I was at Waresley I never danced with anyone else, which was quite false, so now they all laugh at me about it; my love for Teddy has rather gone down. Tomorrow being Mr. Peel's birthday, we are to go to Waresley and have a nice little dance, which will be very nice. I believe the little Bakers are to be there, which I am very glad of, as they will make some nice partners for me.

Thursday, 22nd August. Today Mr. Peel is 46 years old I believe. We had capital fun at the ball, if so it may be called, at Mr. Peel's. We went about 9 o'clock, the Bakers came in just afterwards, and I suppose we began dancing about half past 9. We danced Quadrilles, Waltzes, 5 or 6 Polkas, 2 or 3 Lancers, Boulanger, Mazurka. I did not dance the Mazurka as I do not know it, but it seemed to be very easy. I do not much like being so much flattered when I dance, there is always "This is my favourite partner", "This little girl dances it the best", "You always know everything perfectly", "How very prettily you dance it" going on. I like a little of it but not so much. Robert always makes me dance with those horrid Mr. Leas, who certainly do smell most dreadfully of snuff and tobacco. I danced first a quadrille with young Percival, a very stupid long legged dull man. (I have just remembered that it was another dance I danced with Percival, and this I danced with Frederic Baker.) The second dance was a Polka, which I did not dance as Mama does not like us to dance it with gentlemen except brothers and cousins, though I do not see more harm in that than in a Galop. The next was the Lancers, which I believe I danced with Percival and of course all the others but Mr. Niven and I made a horrid mess of it. The next was a Waltz which of course I did not dance as I do not know how. The next was another Quadrille which I danced with John Lea, who I cannot bear, and is very vulgar and stupid and short. The next was another Polka which I danced with Herbert, and Mrs. Peel said as we went by "I never saw anything so pretty". The next was a Galop, which I did not dance, and Herbert and Miss Dudley Percival, and I believe they were rather laughed at. The next was another Quadrille, which I danced again with that horrid Percival, as Robert always comes up and says "Emily, will you dance with young Percival". The Talbots came in just after that, and she danced the Polka with Henry, this Polka I did not dance, and Mrs. Talbot danced it very bad, and thought she danced it very well. The next was the Mazurka, which of course I did not dance, as I do not know. Robert was bothering everybody to dance, but very few people could. The next was a Boulanger, which I danced with Mr. Talbot, who could not dance it a bit, and kept pulling me round as he did not know what to do. After that supper came, and I was afraid Mr. Talbot would take me in to supper, so I said "Let us

[41]

go to Mama" and as soon as we got there, he said "I am afraid my partner wants to get rid of me". Then we went into supper, and I walked in with Louisa, and got next to Mr. Talbot! There was one amusing anecdote, viz: The servant came up and said "Your plate please sir". Mr. Talbot was talking so I just took his plate and gave it to the servant. He turned round and said "Thankyou ma'am", and afterwards I found out he had not finished. It was a capital joke at the time! There were a great many toasts and speeches. After supper we had another Polka, which I danced first with Jane then with Herbert, then with Louisa. Minnie polked with Miss Baker, she asked if she danced it well, as she wanted her to dance gentleman, so Miss Baker puts on a very gracious smile and says "They tell me so"! Another Waltz, which I did not dance. Another Quadrille which I danced with Mr. Niven, he made me another compliment and said "This is my favourite partner". Another Polka which I don't remember, then the Lancers which I danced with Mr. Pakington, who was the nicest partner I had. Miss Peel was my viz-a-viz, which I liked very much. I did not dance with Herbert Peel once, and only once with Frederick Baker. They all three talked together, and never spoke once. Altogether I enjoyed it very much and of course was very sorry to come away.

Friday, 23rd August. Today the Disbrowes went away which I was very sorry for, as I am very fond of Jane, and of them all. Lady Disbrowe gave me a little tiny wooden lobster, the tail of which unscrewed and a little tiny wooden man came out fastened to the tail. I was very sorry when they went.

Saturday, 24th August. Today the Tylers went at 8 o'clock I was very sorry for that too! It is settled that I am to write a long account to Harriet of anything particular that happens and she is to do the same to me. I am so very sorry that everybody is gone, we have nothing to look forward to except Mama's going away, which I shall not like at all as she is going for 3 nights. I wish Mrs. Peel would ask us to stay at Waresley while she was gone, and then I should not mind it near so much. When Jane was here, we settled to write to each other, but I do not think we shall, as I think she will not like it. The other day I had a letter from Mrs. S. Sullivan, instead of Harriet, as she could not write well enough. It was a very nice letter. I am always laughed at for having so many correspondents, but as I like writing and receiving answers very much, I do not see much harm in it, and I think it is a very nice way of keeping up friendship. I have at present if every body writes that ought — Jane — Harriet Sullivan — Harriet Tyler — Mary — and all the other Tylers. I am sorry to say the poor woman at the turnpike is dead. I do not know what will become of the poor little baby. I believe the school here is soon to put out of Chancery, and then I hope Aunt Harriet will let Teddy and Hubby come there, as they can always come down here on a half-holiday, which I think would be very delightful. I am sorry to say I forgot to send my love to any of them when Aunt Harriet went away, so I am afraid Teddy will forget me. Whenever there is any chance of seeing him again, my love always comes back again, so now there is a chance of his coming to the school I long to see him again. The only time I ever really lost my heart was to Villiers Lister, a very handsome boy about 11 years old, with long curls, but though I have ever since, and I daresay shall for ever like him very much, yet the actual love only lasted 1 night. I remember I told him he should see me at the riding-school when Louisa went, but Louisa did not go, so I did not, and he did not see me. I do not know whether he cared or not I am sure. I believe his real love is a certain Amelia Berkeley who I met at the same dance. I was at Mrs. Drummond, the mother of our friend Mary, that I met them. There are two or three generations of Listers, that is to say from a different wife, but this Villiers is a son of Lady Theresa Lister, and has a very nice little sister, about 9 years old, her name is Theresa, but she is called Toddles. As this is all a long description about a boy and his relations I shall now pass on to

Sunday, 25th August. A tolerably fine day. Went to Church had a pretty good sermon from Mr. Baker, which I did not pay much attention to, as I was thinking about the Peels, and wondering whether they would ask us to their house, when Mama went away as she did last year. When I came

home I asked Louisa if she would like to go and she said "Not at all" which I wondered at as she liked it very much last year, but when I asked she could only say that she thought she would be very much bored, so altogether I am afraid we shall not go. Poor Hamlet (one of the horses) is sentenced to be shot, as he has strained his back, and is not fit for anything. I am sorry, as we have had him some time. Burgess told me last night that the Peels admired the four Miss Tylers very much indeed! and Loudy looked so nice that we women hardly knew her.

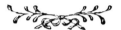

Monday, 26th August. Today we were up and began lessons regularly which I do not much like. At present I do French exercises for ¾ hour, Maps 1 hour, Music 1¼, read French and English ¾ hour, write French Copy ½ hour. I liked doing Maps very much; they are traced out, and one only has to put the names in and paint it. I have made this description in case I get married and have children it may be useful to them. I remember Mama often tells us of what she used to do, she said there were hardly any children's books then and she astonished me the other day by saying she had never read the "Child's Own Book"! I was looking in Mama's trunk for something the other day and the first thing I saw was, at the top of a great many Journal books or something of that sort a piece of paper on which was written "If I die, let these be burnt", and something else which I did not see! I am sure I should like to see them very much, and I do not see why they should be burnt. This morning we resumed our Archery, but I did not get in once. Henry got rather exasperated, because he did not shoot very well. In the afternoon Mama and I went to the school. One of the children has been very irregular, consequently she was sent away today. I must say I think Mama does much more good to the school than Mrs. Baker. After that we strolled about the park and then came in rather tired. I long for Aunt Jane and her children to come here; she has got one girl very much about my age, and I am rather anxious to know her; she has one boy, about 16 who is half silly, and another little boy. Emy is the name of her girl, she is rather older than me. I heard something of her from the Tylers. Aunt Jane is coming some time in September I believe.

Tuesday, 27th August. This afternoon Papa, Mama and I went to Norchard (the name of a little hamlet where a certain Mrs. Clark lives) to give Mrs. Clark her baby clothes; her present baby is too old I should think, but it will do for the next one, if she has another. We have been meaning to go for a long time, but something has always prevented us till today. I do so like going among poor people if they are clean and do not cry as some do, but this Mrs. Clark is as clean and nice as anyone can be; it is a very small poky little cottage with two rooms, and she pays 5£ year, she has 6 children at home and 1 out. I should very much like to buy something more for the poor people, but as I have not got a halfpenny at present it is impossible; there is not much chance of getting anything either for if I say to Mama "I have not got a halfpenny" she says "No worse than me", as she spent all hers in London; I do not think I shall get much next year as I do not expect to have much from my allowance this year, but I should like to do something more about the poor people. I must persuade Teddy to be a clergyman, if he ever means to be my husband, for I have quite set my heart upon being a clergyman's wife or the wife of an independent gentleman; the last I should not in the least object to, as I could do just as much good among the poor people. We were talking today of Papa's being made Archbishop of Canterbury, that is the only thing I should like if he left here, except Winchester, and I do not think I should object to that, though I do not suppose my opinion would be asked. I should not like to go to London at all, and Canterbury is what I should like best. Papa says he would not refuse London if offered to him. I wish I had a little money now, as I am full of the poor people. I think if I do not see Teddy soon I shall give him up, as there is no use loving a boy one is never to see. It would seem by this as if I did not love him much, but really I think if I was to see him again my love would all return, as it is not near gone yet. In fact I still like him very much indeed, and if he comes to the school here I shall love him as much as ever again if he still cares for me; he has not written to me for a long time. I expect and hope Jane will write soon, as I do not think I can well write to her till she has written to me. Mama had a letter from Aunt Harriet this morning, she crossed safely and all are well.

Wednesday, 28th August. A beautiful day. This morning we went out shooting; that is to say Henry and Louisa did, for Herbert and I were looking for our arrows which we lost the other day but did not find them. As Herbert broke his bow the other day, it was sent to Worcester today to be mended, so I lent Herbert my bow for a little while, but no sooner did he begin shooting than he broke one of my arrows, my bow being so much weaker than his he stretched it even beyond the arrow so the arrow flew back and broke. Then after that Herbert laid my bow under the target thinking it would be a safe place, but the first shot of Henry's went underneath, and chipped a piece clean out, so that my bow is hardly fit for use, but I daresay it will last a little longer. Loudy and Henry shot very well. In the afternoon we were to have gone to a cricket match there is on the common today between Worcestershire and Shropshire, but Herbert did not like it as the Peels and Bakers were to be there, which is just the part I should like, but he never likes that sort of thing, so I gave up to him and we did not go, but I was rather disappointed when Mama came up and said "O I daresay he would do it if you liked" but never said anything to me for having given up to him, and I am sorry to say I do a great many more things for the praise of Mama than for the love of God, but I hope I shall improve by degrees. I always feel a degree of pleasure in doing anything right, but never feel as happy as I think I ought to do. Today Mr. Granville Yorke came. He is a very nice funny man. We used to know him at Westmill very well. He has now got the living of St. Philip's Birmingham, which will be nice and close, though 30 miles off. He has got several very nice little children which must be much altered since we were at Westmill. As far as I remember I like them all very much. I hope he and all his party will come some day and stay here a short time.

Thursday, 29th August. An intensely hot day. In the morning we shot and I got one arrow into the target. I wish I could find the one I have lost, and mend that one that is broken. In the afternoon Papa, Mr. Yorke, Mama and I started to go by the wood and home by the common which Mama and I did, but Papa and Mr. Yorke went round by the [. . .] and of course were very hot and tired, and even we on that broiling common nearly had coup-a-soleils, it was so hot, even Mama said she had never felt so hot in her head before. The riders were very hot too. Tomorrow we are to go to a concert, and I rather dread sitting backwards, with the sun shining full upon you and feeling very uncomfortable, but I think the concert will make up for it. We are to hear Salvi, Persiani, Fornosari, and somebody else.

Friday, 30th August. This afternoon we went to the said Concert which I enjoyed very much as I am very fond of music. Orsini (the man which I have put down as "somebody else") accompanied, and sung a little, but very little: he could not sing a bit. Mama liked Salvi the best, and I do not think I much care between Salvi and Fornosari, the former had the best voice and the latter amused me most. There were some very funny songs that he and Persiani sung together, and they both laughed in time. They were all in Italian, but we had a translation in our books, so we knew what made them laugh. They sang "Di capricci", "Non piu Andrai" "Ciel pietosa" and "Pappa---" which was a very funny song indeed, and Fornosari sang it very well. Persiani sang very well, but strained her voice rather too much. Mama talks of nothing but Salvi. The Peels did not go, as they thought it was too hot, so there was only Robert Peel and his friends there of the family. The room was quite crowded, it was in the Natural History Room, which is used for all sorts of things. As we came home we saw Herbert Peel riding, with his servant riding close behind him, for fear he should tumble off I suppose "poor little fellow, it would be a pity for anything to happen to him" the Peels would say. Though I am very fond of the Peels yet I think they are rather foolish as to their children, — for instance — Augusta dresses just as if she was out — Robert keeps his own valet and when he goes to Oxford Mrs. Peel pays all his expenses — Herbert goes out riding and has a servant to ride behind him, and keeps a donkey-cart. These are all the particulars I remember at present.

Saturday, 31st August. This morning I did not feel well, as I felt very sick and rather a head-ache, but when Mama came down I told her, as she is always so very kind to me. I was very sorry it happened today as dear Mama goes away for three nights, which is rather a long time for her, but she always leaves us Nana who takes very good care of us, and understands all about medicine and stuff. She is a very dear goodnatured creature, and we are all very fond of her, but still I cannot bear Mama's going away, as she is the best friend I have on earth, and she is as good a Mother as ever existed. She is going to [write to] us if she has time, and I am to write to her tomorrow. She is going for two nights to Mrs. Essington's at Malvern, and then she is going for one at Mrs. Galton's, so that makes 3 nights. Mr. Essington is quite laid up from his cowardly behaviour viz: the gig ran away and Mr. Essington jumped out and hurt himself dreadfully, she very courageously fell down upon her knees and seized hold of the reins, which she pulled as hard as she could, but of course she could not hold the horse in, who tried to jump over the turnpike gate and of course broke the gig to pieces and poor Mrs. Essington was in it, but I believe she was not much hurt. I have had a nice dose of Jalop today, which I did not much like, but I am getting used to taking those horrid things. Louisa has just been very illnatured viz: Herbert having done something tiresome I called him some name, which Louisa immediately wrote down in her Journal, which was very illnatured, as I only said it in fun.

September
1844

Sunday, 1st September. Today as we had no Mama, Louisa heard us our Catechism &c., which I never like so much, as she does not understand the reading so well. We went to Church where we surprised to see a strange man walk up to the reading-desk instead of Mr. Niven, but we soon found out that it was a brother of Mr. Baker, who was staying in the house. I never like a Sunday without Mama and I was thinking today if the same thing was to happen to her, that happened to Mrs. Essington. Today I wrote to her, which I always like doing to her, and I hope we shall hear from her tomorrow. The wasps bothered us dreadfully in church, which was very disagreeable. I have never been stung by one yet and I hope I never shall.

Monday, 2nd September. Heard from dear Mama this morning; she arrived safe and is quite well. Louisa is to play me a trick tomorrow morning viz: she says to me "I will make you walk down stairs and out of your room between 3 and 4 o'clock in the morning"; of course at present I cannot make it out at all, but she says she will tell me at breakfast tomorrow. I am very curious to know. This evening Herbert and I played at chess; we played two games and I beat Herbert twice, which of course I wondered at very much, as I do no think I ever beat anybody at chess before. Herbert did not seem to like it much. He said he should not mind it with any other person, but he knew I should tell it "all over Worcester-shire" which of course was not true. The first game was quite an oversight on Herbert's side, but the second was quite fair. I have not told anybody yet, not even Mama, and I do not think he would even like that.

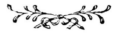

Tuesday, 3rd September. Today we heard again from Mama, as I wrote yesterday. She came home about 12 o'clock this morning. Today Louisa asked me how I liked my walk between 3 and 4 o'clock this morning, which I was rather surprised at, as because I did not much like it she said she would not do it that night, but she did it in the morning. She told me at breakfast how she did it. She writes on one door-post "3" and on the other "4 o'clock in the morning" and then when you go down stairs you go between "3" and "4 o'clock in the morning" as you go between each door-post! On opening the letters when Mama came home there was one from Aunt Harriet, in which she said that Teddy and Hubby went to Mr. Bruce to be taught, so I am afraid there is not much chance of their coming to school here, which I am very sorry for, as I thought we should have such fun together on half holidays. I am afraid now I shall never see him again or not till he has made another love and forgotten all about me, which I rather think he has, as he has not written to me for such a long time. Mama has had another child to put to school. A Mrs. Hopeross's child. I am so very glad Mama has come home again. Today she heard that Mrs. Claughton had got another little girl. This evening Herbert & I played at chess and Herbert beat me this time. It was a very long game indeed.

Wednesday, 4th September. This morning Louisa Herbert and I played at trap-bat and ball, which I like very much, though I did not play very well. This morning Louisa and I had Mr. [. . .] (the Music master) again. In the afternoon Herbert and I played at trap-ball again and I played rather better.

Thursday, 5th September. This morning we played at trap-bat and ball again, and in the afternoon Papa, Mama and I went to Waresley to see another cricket match against the Stourbridge, I believe the latter will win as they have got much the best of it, but Mrs. Peel has kindly asked us to go there tonight for a small dance, which of course we accepted, but Papa and Mama are not asked, which I am rather sorry for, but I do not think there will be many people there. Georgy Baker was much more condescending to me today; she talked to me a good deal. We went to Mrs. Peel's about half past 8, but when we got there, we found that nobody had done dinner as the cricket lasted so long, and after all was not finished, so it was a drawn game; we had very good fun dancing, but we were the only people there, except the Bakers, there were good Polkas, all for Mrs. Talbot's sake, who was staying in the house. Louisa danced with Augusta several times. Before the gentlemen came out of dinner we had several little Polkas by ourselves. I danced one with Georgy Baker, one with Mrs. Talbot and at the particular request of Mrs. Peel, one with Herbert; then after the gentlemen came out we had another Polka, then we had a Quadrille, which I danced with Mr. Niven I think, who amuses me greatly by his "pretty Steps" and Augusta who was our viz-a-viz came up to him, and said "I am always afraid of dancing out of time before you Mr. Niven", as he is so very particular about time, and whenever we dance he is always clapping his hands or stamping his foot, to beat the time, and he does look so very ridiculous. I wonder [he] does it, for everybody must observe it; the next was another Polka, which Mr. Niven asked me to dance with him, which of course I refused, as Mama does not like us dancing it with gentlemen, and then he kept on with some foolish nonsense, saying he thought he was a part of Herbert, and so he might dance it with me! I never heard anything so ridiculous but of course I did not dance it with him; then there was the Lancers, which in the set we were in was composed of gentlemen, except Miss Carliss and I; then we had supper and then we came away, about half past 12, after having had some very good fun indeed. Herbert Peel hurt his hand dreadfully at Cricket this morning; the ball knocked out a piece of his knuckle; he never dances with me now. I liked Augusta very much indeed, and Georgy Baker pretty well, much better than usual.

[51]

Friday, 6th September. Today Mama went to pay a visit at Lady Winnington's, who lives a long way off, so she went to luncheon, and did not come home till late. It was a very hot sultry day.

Saturday, 7th September. This morning it was too wet to do anything but walk about, and in the afternoon Mama and I went into the flower gardens, for her to settle something, as she intends to alter it in the afternoon. This afternoon Mama proposed that Henry, Louisa, Herbert and I should go to Pull Court while they were at Dumbleton, and then they would call for us, as they came back, but it would not do as there was not time for them to leave us at Pull Court while they go on to Dumbleton, so we shall not go after all. At present it is settled that they are to go to Dumbleton (Mrs. Holloway) on Wednesday till Saturday, then they go to Pull Court till Monday, which is a very long time for them to be absent from us. Papa does not seem to think we mind, but dear Mama knows that we do. I do not know why exactly, but we always do, or at least I do, miss them very much.

Sunday, 8th September. This morning when I went down Mama comforted me by saying that she should write to us every day. She seemed to think that I did miss her more than the others, which I certainly think I do, as they always laugh at me, for being melancholy when she goes, but I am so fond of her. Went to church morning and afternoon, another sultry day.

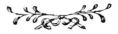

Monday, 9th September. This morning Mama and I went to Lady Harriet Clives at Hewell. She is a very pretty good-natured woman; she has got 6 children, 3 boys and 3 girls all of different ages, the eldest being between 20 and 30, and the youngest being 4. I liked them all pretty well. A very nasty day indeed, cold and foggy.

[52]

Tuesday, 10th September. A tolerably fine day. Henry went out shooting and sprained his ankle getting over a hedge. I believe it was very painful at the time and is still, but I daresay it will soon be better. He *does* look so very funny in his shooting dress. He wears a check frock coat very short — breeches and gaiters, and he looks so funny. In the afternoon Mama and I went to the school, which I always like very much. In the evening Mama, Papa and Henry dined at Mrs. Peel's; I believe it is to be a grand party, as Mr. Peel came this afternoon to ask if we had any ice.

Wednesday, 11th September. Today Mama told us that Mrs. Peel had asked us to go there this evening, which I liked very much, but the others did not much like the thoughts of it. I am always more fond of going out than the others a great deal. At half past 10 dear Mama went away for 5 days. It seems a very long time to us, much longer than it really is. We went to Waresley at 7 and got there full early. We went to dinner. My own brother Herbert took me in, as there was no one else; but on the other side I had Mr. Coventry, who is staying in the house, he is very shy and therefore did not talk much. Altogether I thought rather a dull process, and was glad when it was over. We danced Polkas, Quadrilles, Lancers, Mazurkas, Country dance, Sir Roger de Coverley, and all sorts of dances, and then went to supper, and after supper we had a few more dances and then went away. In the Mazurka there is one figure, where you have to throw up your handkerchief, and who ever catches it leads you to your place. My handkerchief was in my pocket, and I could not get it out in time, at last I did and Louisa who was my partner took me. I wish I had not thrown it up, as it was only a common one, without any lace. Mama does not like us to have lace pocket handkerchiefs, but if she did of course I should not have one as I am too young. She does not like us to carry handkerchiefs, as she thinks it is nasty, but every body does. I danced a Quadrille with Mr. Niven and a Lancers, which I always think a horrid bore. There is a small piece of love going on between Charles Peel (a cousin of our Peels) and Georgy Baker. We had some fun about it, teasing poor Georgy, who got very indignant, I think he is a very nice young man. I set next to him at supper, and he talked to me a great deal.

[53]

We had a few dances after supper and then went away about half past 1. We took Georgy home first and then came here. I like the Peels very much. We were all tired when we came away.

Thursday, 12th September. This morning Henry felt the effects of his evening in feeling sick, and having a head-ache, he had a little ginger-tea at breakfast, which took away his sickness but left his head-ache. We were all rather tired this morning. We played at trap-bat and ball, which made us rather worse. They were all very cross to me, except Herbert, while we were playing. I tried all I could to bowl and catch as well as I could, but they kept saying that I did not try, and that if I did not I should not have my innings. In those cases, when Mama is away, my only comfort is God, and he is a great comfort. I did not know what to do for I could not play better. I wrote to Mama this morning, and I hope I shall hear from her tomorrow. I wrote her a good long letter.

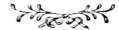

Friday, 13th September. This morning I was very much disappointed to find no letter from dear Mama, but I suppose she had not time, as they went to open some Church yesterday, but I hope I shall hear tomorrow. We shot this morning, but I did not get one arrow into the target. This afternoon Nana Herbert and I had a good game at trap-bat and ball, which made us very hot. I wrote to Mama again today. I generally write as I like it very much, and the others dislike it very much. At present I am reading a very nice book. It is the life of Lord Eldon, but I daresay in a little while it will get too political.

Saturday, 14th September. Today Henry had a letter from Mama and she says she will write to me on Sunday. This afternoon we played at trap-bat and ball for a little time and then we shot [. . .] We were out from 3 till half past 6. Now Mama is away Herbert and I dine with Henry and Louisa every day, which we like very much.

[54]

Sunday, 15th September. In the morning we had a very good sermon from Mr. Baker, I always like his sermons. In the afternoon, a very dull sermon from Mr. Niven, who always preaches very dull. Little Billy (the coachman's child) has just come in, he is such a dear little thing, he is about a year and a half old, he has got a sister named Cary, she is about 5 years old.

Monday, 16th September. In the morning we shot and I got one arrow into the red. About 5 Mama came home, and now we shall be all jolly again, for though we are very happy when she is away, yet we long for her to be home again. In the afternoon we went to Mrs. Peel's to enquire after Miss Peel, Sir Robert Peel's daughter, who has been very ill lately of Scarlet Fever! She is rather better, but still very ill. Mr. Peel went to Canterbury today, and Mrs. Peel and family go on Monday. I shall be very sorry when they are gone, I like them all very much. Today Henry went out shooting with Robert Peel, they are going to some distance and Henry went there at 8. We dine with Mama today.

Tuesday, 17th September. Today Henry went to the Redditch Races. I believe they were very bad. I think Henry seems to like Robert Peel much better than he did. He dined there and slept as it was a very wet night.

Wednesday, 18th September. There was a grand review at Thiempsay today, of all the Yeomanry. It was very pretty and we liked it very much. The Disbrowes were there, as they are staying with the Clives, and we saw Sir Edward and Charlotte. We were to have gone to the Peels tonight, but we could not, as we could not have the horses out again. Henry is going and we are going on Friday. The Disbrowes proposed coming here to luncheon on Friday, and then come here from Saturday till Monday, but I am afraid Jane will not come at all this year. I do not think we shall see her for some years, as they go to the Hague in November. I believe Aunt Jane is coming about the 2nd October.

Thursday, 19th September. A very cold nasty North East wind in the morning, but in the afternoon it was very fine. Mrs. Peel, Augusta and Georgy called this afternoon. Mama told me that when she was at Mrs. Holland's she had almost engaged a French Governess, that is to say, she saw one who she liked very much, and who was going to leave Mrs. Holland, but we should not like it [at] all. Poor Papa has not been at all well today, and he has had a dose, but I daresay he will soon be better.

Friday, 20th September. Today there was another game at cricket at Mr. Peels. I believe Mr. Niven was very cross and ill tempered, but I have not heard the whole history yet. We called at Waresley today, and Mrs. Peel asked Mama to go in the evening, which she did. H. L. H. and I went to dinner at half past 6 Mr. Morant took me in to dinner, he is rather shy, but I liked him very well. The Percivals were there, and of course Georgy was there. Mama went at 9 and we began dancing about half past. The first was a Polka, which I danced with Herbert, though Papa has given us leave to dance it with anybody in such a small party, as they were. The next was a Quadrille which I danced with young Galton, he talked to me a good deal which I liked very much. The next was another Polka which I danced with Herbert, and all the Polkas I danced with him, because Robert kept saying "Now Herbert and Emily you dance it together", so we were obliged. There were two Miss Grays and a Miss Case came in the evening as dancers, and then there was Mrs. Gray, and Mrs. Wyndham, afterwards came Lord Sandys, Major Martin, Colonel Wyndham and Colonel Cheyney. Colonel Wyndham is such an enormous man. They call him the Giant, and I am sure he is very like one. The next dance was a Lancers, which I danced with Mr. Niven, who always engages beforehand, which I do not think is fair, as I do not like dancing with him. Then I think the next was a Waltz which of course I did not dance. Then the next was a Mazurka which I danced with young Percival, so when it came

[56]

to the kneeling down, I gave up my place to Edward Baker, as I knew Percival would be ridiculed, and I did not want to be ridiculed too. I think there was another Polka and then we went to supper. We had two or three more Polkas, one of which I danced with Frederic and Edward Baker, and Augusta said that she thought he was always called Teddy. The only adventure I had was at desert, and that was only helping myself to some grapes, and after fiddling sometime about them I took such a quantity I was so ashamed; we came away about 2. Supper always makes us late. All the Peels go to Canterbury on Monday, as he is Canon of Canterbury. We shall miss them very much as we shall have very few dances, then. I wish Papa was allowed to give dances, but being a Bishop he cannot.

Saturday, 21st September. This morning we were all very tired, as we always are after Mrs. Peel's balls, as we never rest between dances. Louisa and I were up to breakfast, but Henry and Herbert were not down till near half past ten. A very nasty cold day in the morning, but in the afternoon it was very fine. Papa Mama and I took a very nice walk by Whildon, it was rather long for us. I am afraid Mama begins to think seriously about having the French Governess and I am in a dreadful fright.

Sunday, 22nd September. Had a sermon from Mr. Baker which I did not understand, and one from Mr. Niven which I did not like, though Mama said it was a very good one. Somehow I always dislike going to church, and am always glad to get off it if I can. I like it better than I did, so I hope I may like it better still. Yesterday Herbert was very good natured to me.

Monday, 23rd September. Very cold and nasty. In the morning we took a walk by Whildon which is a tin manufactory. It was rather long but I was not very tired. In the afternoon it was very disagreeable indeed, so we did not go out, but Mama went to leave her name at Witley, and

Henry Herbert and I played at "All round my hat" indoors. William Pepys came at half past five. I believe he stays till Monday. I think I rather like him. In the evening Herbert and I played at Chess. A very dull game but Herbert won it.

Tuesday, 24th September. It was very cold, and we played at trap. I play much better than I did I am happy to say, as it is much pleasanter. In the afternoon Herbert and I played again, and Papa, Mama and Louisa went out walking. In the evening we played at Chess again and after several hard battles Herbert beat me again.

Wednesday, 25th September. A very thick fog in the morning, but afterwards it cleared up, and became very fine. Today Papa, Mama and Louisa went to Lady Pepys at Cheltenham. She is an Aunt of Papa's. They come back on Friday. It is the first time of Louisa's "going out" though she does not "come out" till next year. In the afternoon we played at our usual games, and then came in pretty tired, I already begin to long for Mama to come back again. In the evening we talked about a little dance that we are to have on Saturday.

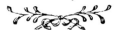

Thursday, 26th September. This morning we did not go out, as it the grass was too wet to play at anything, so we mended old things. In the afternoon we played, and Herbert was very good-natured to me. After that we found a Classical Dictionary in Papa's library which amused us very much.

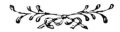

Friday, 27th September. This morning Mama is to come home. I wrote to her yesterday, and she wrote to me today a good long letter, and a very nice one. She came about half past one and we were very glad to see her back again. Today Henry and William went to part of Lady Wood Manor to shoot upon: they took such a luncheon as I never saw before. I hope they will shoot something for their trouble. Mama and Louisa

[58]

bought Herbert's present at Cheltenham. Mama is going to pay my share as I am "hard up".

Saturday, 28th September. Today the Disbrowes come to stay till Monday. I am very glad as I like Charlotte very much. I am only so sorry Jane cannot come, as she is my friend. When Louisa was at Cheltenham she bought a pair of very funny curling-irons. They had a little comb fastened to it, and a little spring which pushed the comb in when you pulled it out of your hair. Today we called at Mrs. Claughton's, and met them just at their gate Lady Ward, Mrs. Claughton and their eldest child, who is about 1 year and a half old. A most beautiful day. Mama had a very bad head-ache. Lady Disbrowe went this afternoon to leave her name at Witley, and she thinks if she is asked to dine there of coming again for that night, and then Herbert and I shall have to amuse them. I should like it but I am sure Herbert would not. This evening we had a small dance. Messrs. Baker and Niven, Mrs. Baker and Georgy Baker. First we had a Polka which I danced with Herbert, next a Lancers which I danced with Herbert, then a Waltz which I did not dance, then a Quadrille which I danced with Mr. Niven but which I ought to have danced with William as Henry had written it all down on paper, but as I did not remember at the time I danced with Mr. Niven, but of course I would much rather have danced it with William, the next was a Polka which I danced with Herbert, then a Lancers which I danced with William to make amends for my "cutting" him before. Then a Waltz which I did not dance, and then Sir Roger de Coverley, which I danced with Mr. Niven. Then the Bakers went away so our dance broke up. After the Lancers William and I had a nice little walk in the Gallery which I liked very much, and I like him very much too. Henry and Georgy had a long private walk and talk in the Gallery and I think a small piece of flirtation is going on between those two, but still I do not see how it can be as her affections are bestowed on Charles Peel, but perhaps she is not constant. I liked everybody and everything, but never laughed so much before at little Mr. Niven as I did then. He figured and stepped away like an Opera dancer. I liked Georgy very much as I always have lately.

[59]

Sunday, 29th September. This morning Mr. Claughton preached a charity sermon for the benefit of the Sunday schools. I believe they got about £26 10s. but I believe that was not much as the church holds 15 hundred I believe. Mr. Baker preached in the afternoon. They were both very good sermons but I think for once I liked Mr. Claughton's the best.

Monday, 30th September. Today the Disbrowes and William went away, and I must say I was more sorry for the latter than the former as I liked William very much. I believe he will come back at Christmas. He was very sorry to go too, poor fellow. He told Henry he had enjoyed his visit so very much, but he and Henry will soon meet again at Cambridge. If Jane had been here I daresay I should have been more sorry for the Disbrowes. Today also Mama, Papa Henry and Louisa went to Hewell so altogether I am rather melancholy today. Mama comes back on Wednesday so that we have not long to wait. I am afraid Mama has really serious thought about that French Governess which I mentioned before. I am sure I hope from my very heart she will not get her, as I should think it such a bore. I wish Mama did not go out so much and then we should not want one. Last night we had great fun, viz: Lady Disbrowe told us to take a sheet of paper which we did, then she told us what to write upon it such as "Put down a single lady's name" or "Name a number of years" or anything like that and after it was all done she had piece of paper and questioned us such as to the first question I put she asked What is the name of your admirer, or something like that, and then what you had put upon paper answered.

October
1844

Tuesday, 1st October. Being a very damp nasty day, we did not go out but Herbert went on with his box, which he began making some time ago, and I began one but did not succeed as the wood broke. I wrote to Mama. In the afternoon we set about our boxes again and I got on beautifully. Both were very good-natured to each other.

Wednesday, 2nd October. Today Mama came home about 1 and of course we were very glad. At about 5 Aunt Jane came with her children Augustus 17, Emy 13 and Frederick 9. I believe they are going to stay till next Wednesday. I did not much like the looks of Emy, but in the evening I liked her better. Frederick seems a very nice little boy. In the evening we taught Augustus the Polka, but he does not know it well. I think Emy is rather affected, which in my opinion is a great fault.

Thursday, 3rd October. Papa and Mama went to Worcester to hear a Charity Sermon. Emy and I played at Coronella in the morning and in the afternoon Lady Kilmaine and Louisa Disbrowe came to stay for a week. Yesterday Uncles George and John came, so our house is pretty full. Yesterday evening our long-expected Bantams arrived. They are a present from Miss Lechmere to Herbert and I. They are very pretty indeed. We give them to old Betty to take care of. I do not much like Emy as she is affected and seems to be very fond of dress, as she dresses as if she was

[61]

out. We had another dance tonight, which principally consisted of Polkas. I like Louisa Disbrowe very much indeed, she seems to be full of fun. She is rather pretty, but not very. I do not think Papa much likes our dancing. He does not even like our having Georgy Baker.

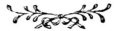

Friday, 4th October. This morning Herbert and I made Emy, Augustus and Frederick all get out of their room between 3 and 4 o'clock in the morning. Herbert propose not rubbing it out, so that every body that sleeps in those rooms must get out of bed between 3 and 4 o'clock in the morning. This afternoon we all took a walk to the Locks and took "Peggy" with us for the tired ones, but though I was very tired I did not like to ride on her as she is too high. Louisa D. got on famously and when Peggy trotted she looked just like an old woman going to market in bonnet and shawl; did not like Emy much, but liked Louisa D. very much. I think I forgot to say that young Mr. and Miss Coventry came Thursday to stay till Saturday. In the evening we danced again and I liked Emy very much indeed. I think that what I thought was affected was only being shy, as she talked to me a great deal, and seemed to like me rather.

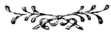

Saturday, 5th October. This morning Louisa D. played to us; she plays very nice indeed, as all her notes are so neat. This evening we did not dance, as Louisa D. was copying out some Waltzs for Louisa. I was trying to find out a trick with numbers which both Henry and Herbert know. This afternoon being a very damp muggy misty, rainy day, we did not go out, but asked riddles and played at Cross Questions and Crooked Answers which is a very nice game, if played well. Poor Augustus could not manage it at all well as he is rather deaf, and it is all done with whispering.

Sunday, 6th October. Today being Sacrament Sunday, Papa preached in the morning and Mr. Baker in the afternoon. Of course after Church in the afternoon we walked round the park, and I have quite altered my opinion of Emy, liking her very much now.

Monday, 7th October. This afternoon we all, that is Lady Kilmaine, Louisa D., Uncle George, Mama, Emy and I in the carriage, and Augustus, Henry, Louisa and I made an expedition to Woodbury Hill, and Louisa D. and Louisa P. were engaged in earnest conversation all the time, and I think and am afraid that it was about Herbert, as from what I could catch up, I heard "He was just the same out-riding" and those sort of things, but I do not know what it was. It was not a very fine day, and very cold, but as we were 6 in the carriage we were not very cold. I like Lady Kilmaine and Louisa D. very much indeed, I think the former is a very wonderful woman to be able to walk up Woodbury Hill at 73 years of age. In the evening we played at the Family Coach which is very good fun indeed; each of you are to be part of the coach, and whenever your name is mentioned, you are to jump up and turn round.

Tuesday, 8th October. This morning Emy and I settled to write to each other, I think I shall have more chance of hearing from her than anyone else, as she rather likes writing. I like her very much, and Freddy is the dearest little boy I ever saw, he is so very good-natured and good-tempered, that it is impossible not to like him. I think he will be very sorry to go poor little fellow, as he seems to dread it very much. They all go tomorrow I am sorry to say. Louisa seems to have made great friends with Louisa D., she always goes upstairs with her, and comes down with her and I think considering they both sleep at different sides of the house that is great nonsense. This evening we danced again as Henry wanted Louisa D. to teach him the "stalking step" which is a step in the Polka, but I do not know how to do it. This evening was a memorable evening insomuch as at tea I cut Herbert's hand and probably he will have the scar all his life. We were playing with him (that is to say Freddy and I) and he was pretending to be asleep, I was going just to touch him with my knife to make him open his eyes, and he pushed his hand back to push me away, and run his hand through my knife, (i.e. so as to make a great gash), he bore it so beautifully too, he only said "O, Emy you had better send for Nana" which of course I immediately did. It did not bleed much fortunately, but Mama thought we had better send for the doctor and

[63]

surgeon at Stourport, namely Mr. Barnett, who came in about an hour. When he came, he put a splint under Herbert's hand and tied it up, and put some kind of plaster upon it, he wanted to sew it up but Mama would not let him. There was a small piece, regularly cut out, so he was obliged to join it together, with this plaster. I was in agony myself, I could not rest without coming to see him every moment, till he was very much better, and then I went down. I was so afraid, it would end in a lock-jaw, but I do not think it will. Of course, Mr. Barnett made quite a case of it, as all doctors do, and he is coming again tomorrow, which I am very glad of as it will make me much more comfortable. I could not dance in any comfort this evening of course, as I was so fidgetty about Herbert. He is so very good-natured about it, not having grumbled once, which I am sure I fully deserved for having been so very careless.

Wednesday, 9th October. Today I was in great perplexity, as I gave up my first music-lesson (being Mr. Done's day) to Louisa, as she wanted to wish people "Goodbye" as much as I did, and one of us I thought must be prevented, but as it happened, I had done before they went, so I wished both Emy (which for the future I shall spell Emie) and Louisa D., which are the two I liked best, Goodbye, which is very pleasant, as there are always a few last words to say. I was very sorry indeed when they went away, as I was very dull indeed. On the whole I liked Emie very much, and all of them. The two Louisas seemed to make great friends, and I liked Louisa D. very much indeed. Tonight I went to bed at 9, which I have not done for some time, and which I do not like doing at all. Herbert's hand is much better today.

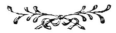

Thursday, 10th October. Today Mama, Papa and Henry went to Eastnor Castle at Lord Somer's to stay till Saturday, but we have Louisa this time, so it is not half so bad. A very tolerable fine day, and much warmer. I believe Mama intends to alter her garden next week, which will be very good fun, but she will not, unless some of the flowers are killed by frost. Herbert's hand is a great deal better today, but he has still got his arm in a sling, and his hand bound up. Mr. Barnett comes again tomorrow, and I hope Herbert will soon be pretty well. I am sure I never was so sorry as I was about it, as it seemed so careless, and as I had often been told not to play with knives. This afternoon it was warm enough to sit out. In the morning we went in the boat which came the other day. It is a very nice one indeed, and very safe.

Friday, 11th October. A very showery day, but we got out between the showers. The boat-house is preparing to be built, but it is not begun yet. Mr. Niven came to enquire about Herbert's hand. Mr. Barnett came in the morning. I am sorry to say I do not think his hand is quite so well as it was yesterday. It is so dreadfully swelled, but I hope it will soon be better. Louisa and Herbert were rather cross to me this morning, but were much better in the afternoon, so I suppose it was partly my fault. I wrote to Mama today, and I hope I shall hear from her tomorrow morning. In the afternoon we could not go out, as it rained all the time, but looked in Papa's library for a book of pictures, which we did not find after all. We feel very dull after both Disbrowes and Sullivans and Papa, Mama and Henry are gone, but I daresay we shall soon have it full again.

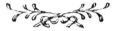

Saturday, 12th October. This morning we went out, though it was not very fine, we went to see how the boat-house is getting on. It is hardly begun yet as they are letting off the water. He is going to build it in a very awkward place as it is the other side of the water. Mr. Niven came again today to enquire about Herbert's hand. He seems very kind to him. He always stays such a long time when he does come. This afternoon Mama came about 3, and I believe she wrote to us but we never received it, so I suppose it will come tomorrow. Of course I am very glad Mama is come home again, and I hope now she will not go to sleep out again. Not a very nice day, but very warm and mild. We walked about the garden in the afternoon and came in about 6. Herbert's hand is better today.

[65]

Sunday, 13th October. Had a good sermon from Mr. Baker in the morning and a dull one from Mr. Niven in the afternoon. A very disagreeable wet day. Herbert left off his sling and bandage today, and only keeps on his sticking plaster, with another plaster under it.

Monday, 14th October. A very disagreeable rainy damp muggy wet dirty day, and altogether the most disagreeable day I was ever in. We went in the boat in the morning, but it kept raining every minute, and then as soon as we had got out of the boat, which was no small trouble, it left off raining, and then we got in again. I steered at first, and then pulled a little, the latter I could not manage well at first trial. Henry grumbles at my steering but I do not think I do it so very bad after all. I caught two crabs, which is very disagreeable.

Tuesday, 15th October. Another very rainy disagreeable day, but we managed to get out in the afternoon, and visit a poor woman who has been very ill, Louisa and I did not go in as Papa did not like it, Henry and Herbert went in the dearly beloved boat in the afternoon but Papa thought it was too damp for Louisa and I, so Papa, Mama Louisa and I went out to visit this poor woman. In the morning we could not go out, as it rained so. I have begun making a new silk apron for myself, as Mama wants us to learn needle-work. The leaves are coming off dreadfully and Papa says that if he had his whole income i.e. what the other Bishops used to have, he would go to the sea-side at this time of year, as he says it is so unwholesome when the leaves are coming off.

Wednesday, 16th October. This morning we went in the boat, which I liked very much. At first Henry sculled and broke one of the sculls. The water is very low, as it has been let off, for the boat-house to be made. I pulled a little this morning. Herbert's hand is getting much better now, he has only got a small piece of stinging-plaster on now.

[66]

Thursday, 17th October. This morning Henry went back to Cambridge. I am not very sorry, as when he is at home he is always very cross and ill-natured to me, but I think he improves in good-nature. This afternoon we took a walk on the common. I am afraid now Henry is gone, we shall hardly ever go in the boat, as we are not allowed to go in by ourselves, and I do not think Papa will often go with us, as he is generally busy.

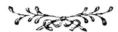

Friday, 18th October. In the morning we went out, but as we could not go in the boat, we had nothing to do, and Herbert had gone to Worcester. Yesterday at luncheon Papa said that Henry was going to get Herbert's and my January present as he went through London. He said that Herbert's and mine were to be the same, by which we conjecture that it is one of the games they had at Eastnor, such as Chinese Billiards and Bagatelle, or some of those sort of things. I rather wish it was not to be between us.

Saturday, 19th October. This morning we did not go out as it rained, nor in the afternoon till about 4 o'clock, when we staid out till 5. Minnie Stuart sent us a new Polka this morning which Louisa is copying out. I believe it is one Lady Waterford brought from Ireland. It is pretty, but I do not think it is a very good one to dance to. I have been copying out a piece of music for Mama and I like copying very much.

Sunday, 20th October. This morning I was not well, as I am cutting my 12 year old teeth. At breakfast my tooth hurt me dreadfully, then I had a head-ache, and then I felt sick, so I did not feel at all equal to going to church, so Mama gave me a nice dose of Jalop instead of taking it in the next morning, which was what she intended at first. We had 3 or 4 very loud claps of thunder, followed by a very sharp hail storm, in the afternoon, just as they were coming from church. Mama got finely blowed, actually having to run all the way from Betty's lodge to the house. Of course I did not go to church either morning or afternoon.

[67]

Monday, 21st October. Today the operations in the garden commenced, such as taking down "one very large, untidy, ugly Portugal Laurel", which grows in the garden, taking up some *Misembrisanthemums* (I do not think I have spelt it right but it is the name of a flower), and measuring a little, but Mama having got a bad cold in her head, and going to dine at the Queen Dowager's at Witley, before whom she is not allowed to sneeze or blow her nose, she was nursing this said cold, and therefore did not go out, and therefore there was not much done, but I hope tomorrow we shall begin in good earnest, only that are some more company coming.

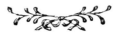

Tuesday, 22nd October. This morning we cut some sticks for Mama to alter the garden, which she did in the afternoon, that is to say she pegged out the shape of her beds in which we did most as she [had] only one of the gardeners to take up some flowers. Mrs. and Miss Vansittart came today, and Mr. Grantham Yorke. We rather expected the Queen today, but she did not come.

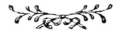

Wednesday, 23rd October. Today we did not do anything in the garden, as company interfered and did not go out, as it was very foggy in the morning, but in the afternoon we went round the park and as we were with an old lady, i.e. Mrs. Vansittart we walked very slow, and then went to see the church and met Mr. Baker who showed us (who had of course seen it very often before) and the company the church, he showed us the organ, that is to say he did not open, but showed us the outside and the place where the singers sat, where we had never been before. I do like Mr. Baker so very much, and he does preach such excellent sermons, they are the only sermons I ever like. I used to think Papa's were the best, but they are nothing to Mr. Baker's. Today the Pearson's dined here, and Mr. Baker. Mama and Mr. Yorke sang some duets, and Louisa played her duet with Mama.

Thursday, 24th October. It rained all day, in the morning Miss Vansittart played us some Polkas, that Minnie Stuart sent us. The two last are very pretty, and those are the two I am going to copy. In the afternoon I had a famous game at "Battledore and Shuttlecock" with Mr. Yorke; we had very good fun indeed, as we played rather boisterously, and then had a small game at Coronella with him, which he did not like much. At present Louisa and I are copying out a Waltz of Miss Vansittart, which I finished in the evening, and then began copying out one of Polka's. Mr. Hastings and Mr. Niven dined here tonight, and I believe Mama hurt poor little Snivens feelings in saying that she intended Herbert to go to Mr. Alford's when he was 16, if he was not made Bishop of New Brunswick, which I believe has been offered to him (By Sniven I mean Mr. Niven, but that is the nickname we give him).

Friday, 25th October. Today the Vansittarts went; also Mr. Yorke and Mr. Murray (I think I forgot to say that Mr. Murray came yesterday). Therefore we are quite alone for the present. This afternoon Mama and I went to call on Lady Barrington, at Witley, who is the lady in waiting, but she was not at home, and so we did not see anyone. Mrs. Baker and Miss Cooke called today.

Saturday, 26th October. Today we were all busy in the garden, and so I am *very* tired, as I have been working hard all the afternoon. I think I have been working the hardest, as Herbert has only got one hand that he can use, and Louisa went about measuring with Mama. Mama of course did not do any hard work. Herbert and I did all that. I took up some flowers with a *"pick-axe"* and then cut some turf, which was very hard work, as it hurt my foot so pushing the spade in, as that was the only instrument I had for it. Altogether I am almost too tired to write this. A very wet day, i.e. the morning.

Sunday, 27th October. A very nasty day indeed, but we did manage to go to church both morning and afternoon. Mr. Baker's sermon was not quite so good this morning as it generally is. Papa told Sam (the gardener) to go to the farm, while we were at church, to see if anybody came, as last Sunday we lost a guinea-fowl, and some of Charles' rabbits have been very often taken. One every Sunday regularly.

Monday, 28th October. Today we have been very busy indeed all day in the garden. We went out at half past ten and came in at 2, went out quarter past 3 came in at 5, so we were out nearly all day, and I am rather tired but not very. The garden of course is getting on very nice, and we all think it very good fun altering it, even the gardeners I should think. Herbert's hand heals very slowly, not half so quick as it ought. Mr. Barnett still comes every other day.

Tuesday, 29th October. Today also we have been very busy in the garden, and I think in about 2 more days we shall have done all the "sticking". Papa is the person who interferes most about it, as he never liked the altering at all, and Mama has done all she can to please, and he rather grumbles. We had (that is Mama had) a letter from Henry this morning, and there was some secret in it, which we suppose was something about Herbert's and my January present. There was also a long letter from Miss Vansittart, giving a long account of poor Theresa Drummond who has been very ill indeed lately, and I believe the doctors say it will be three months before she is well again, but I believe she is better; also sending Herbert a book called Baron Munchausen, which was very kind of her. It is a very funny book, which we have wanted to have for some time, but could not get it.

Wednesday, 30th October. Today we did not go in the garden at all as it was very wet and Mama did not want to tire herself before her company come, who came at about 5, the Bishop of Hereford and Mrs. Musgrave, Mr. Raimont, and Mr. and Lady Margaret Cocks, all to stay till Friday or Saturday, and Sir Offley Wakeman. Mrs. Musgrave seems to be a very nice lady-like person, though she did not shake hands with me, but he did and he is only a tailor's son. I had a letter from Hubby Tyler this morning, but I have not heard from Teddy for a long time. It was a much nicer letter than he usually writes, as there was much more sense in it. He begs I will answer it soon; I have not heard from Emie Sullivan at all yet, and I cannot think why. Tonight I played my Duet with Mama, but did not get through it very well, but Mr. Niven admired it because I played in time and he has got a very good ear.

Thursday, 31st October. Today the Bishop of Hereford went to consecrate some church near here, and Mama, Mrs. Musgrave, Lady M. Cocks and I went to call on Mrs. Claughton, and saw the dearest little child, about 1½ year old. It runs about the room and can speak tolerably well. I like both Mr. and Mrs. Claughton very much, and also I like little children very much. Today was Herbert's birthday and we gave 2 very nice games one was called "Storming the Fortress" and the other "The Marksman". Storming the Fortress is much the best, and is something like German Tactics. It is played by cannons, that is sham ones, which one person has, and the other has the little man in the middle. It is like the people and officers in German Tactics. The other, the Marksman, is all chance, and therefore not so nice. Mr. and Mrs. Seymour came today with Mr. Wakeman, a brother of Sir Offley Wakeman.

November
1844

Friday, 1st November. I wrote to Hubby Tyler today, as he asked me to answer his letter soon. The Seymours went away today, and Sir Offley Wakeman, and the Dean of St. Asaph; tomorrow the Musgraves go and then I think we shall be quiet for some time. We took a walk to the Locks today, and Mrs. Musgrave and Lady M. Cocks went to leave their names at Witley.

Saturday, 2nd November. Today the Musgraves and Cocks went away. Mr. Cocks bought Brenda, and I believe she is now under good hands, as he understands horses very well. Papa gave us a job to do in his library as it rained.

Sunday, 3rd November. Another very wet day, but we went to church in the morning, but Herbert and I did not go in the afternoon, and so we went on with the job in Papa's library, which is to arrange some of the books which have got misplaced.

Monday, 4th November. Today Papa Mama and I went to Worcester to do some shopping. I got a new winter frock and some winter gloves, and got Louisa's present and a lantern for Herbert to go to Mr. Niven's. Mama had the Lumbago very bad indeed today.

Tuesday, 5th November. Another very wet day. I really do not know when the wet weather will be over, it has been raining 4 days without stopping except at night. Poor Mama has been very unwell indeed today; she took some Calomel last night and a Black Dose this morning, but the Calomel made her dreadfully sick in the night so that she hardly slept, and the Black Dose not strong enough this morning, so she feels very stupid and not much better, but she still gives a few *"Squeels"* when she moves much. We went on with the books in Papa's library.

Wednesday, 6th November. Another very disagreeable day! though it did not rain quite all day, yet it did most of the morning and all the afternoon. Miss Onerton (the dressmaker) came here today, to make one of my frocks, but I am not to have it till Tuesday. I was to have had it made long, and so without trowsers, but Mama thought I had better wait till spring frocks come into fashion again. I wrote to Emie Sullivan the other day, and I suppose I shall hear soon, Herbert wrote to Freddy too. Today we played at the "Sham Fight", which is a very nice game; you fight with "Peas" and little cannons, and there are several small men. Papa went to consecrate some church today, and comes home tomorrow, so Herbert and I dine with Mama tonight. We did the garden this morning, though it rained nearly all the time. Mama is a great deal better today, but not quite well yet.

Thursday, 7th November. Today beautifully fine, but as Mama and Louisa had taken [. . .] the night before, we could not go in the garden before luncheon, but did after, and got on beautifully. We have nearly marked out all the beds now and a great many are cut out and finished. I heard from Emie this morning, and Herbert from Freddy. Mine was a particularly nice letter, and very well written. I think now I shall hear from her very often.

Friday, 8th November. Rained all the morning, and was very wet and damp all the afternoon, so that we did not do much of the garden all day. We tried in the afternoon, but found it so very wet under foot, that we were obliged to leave off and take a walk. On coming home, we were surprised to see that one of our Bantams have laid one egg, and now I suppose it will go on laying every day, and then it will sit and then Herbert and I shall have some young Bantams.

Saturday, 9th November. Today we have been very busy in the garden, and got on famously with it, but were all very tired when we came in. Mama had a letter from Aunt Harriet today, saying that Gwinnett had gone off in a great hurry on board the "Hecta" steamer to Gibralter. I believe it is a very good thing for him. We were in the garden today from 12 in the morning till 5 in the afternoon only coming in for dinner.

Sunday, 10th November. Rained most part of the day, but managed to go to church in the morning, but in the afternoon none of us could but Papa, so Herbert and I went on with his books. Herbert and I hardly ever quarrel now and are great friends.

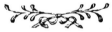

Monday, 11th November. A beautiful day in the morning, but it was too swampy (having rained all night) for us to do anything in the garden, but in the afternoon being much dryer we got out, but it rained all the last part. We have nearly finished it now, and I think it will look much prettier when it is done than it did before. Herbert and I finished Papa's books this morning. Papa went to Worcester today and brought home for me some books and a pair of kid gloves.

Tuesday, 12th November. A very foggy muggy damp rainy day in the morning, but it cleared up in the afternoon, and we went out. Mama and I went to the School, and the others to Stourport. The woman who we went to see is found out to be an impostor, and I believe when she was

[74]

here she got about £2.5.0. but there is no doubt that she was very ill indeed. Mr. Baker is very sorry indeed about it. Miss Lea was married today to a Mr. Heming. She is the daughter of a retired Carpet manufacturer, and he is a needle manufacturer.

Wednesday, 13th November. Poured all morning but cleared up in the afternoon as usual. Of course we can do nothing in the garden such weather, as it is all in a swamp. Mama had a letter from the music-master this morning saying that he was suffering under a bad cold and therefore could not attend his young pupils this morning, which of course we were very glad of. Such a very bad day put me in ill-humour and I was very cross.

Thursday, 14th November. Today was Henry's birthday, but being at Cambridge of course we could not give him any presents, but I wrote to him. Papa and Mama went to Hagley (Lord Lyttelton's), and come back on Saturday. It did not rain in the morning, so we went in the garden, and now we have done pegging out the beds. It rained all the afternoon. Mama went at 4 o'clock P.M. I thought she had done with going out for this year.

Friday, 15th November. Today I wrote two letters, which is a great deal for me. I wrote one to Mama and one to Emie. I like writing letters very much, and I do not think I write very bad for my age, though I certainly do not write so well as Emie. This morning the box of books came from Cawthorn's, which we were very glad of, as we are in great want of books. I have chosen Pickwick, as I know I may read that, and the others I may not read till Mama comes home.

Saturday, 16th November. Mama came home about 12 o'clock. Of course we were very glad. Herbert has been very good-natured to me lately.

[75]

Sunday, 17th November. Very fine indeed in the morning, but very foggy indeed in the afternoon. Went to church both morning and afternoon. Today was Louisa's birthday, but it is not to be kept till Tuesday.

Monday, 18th November. Not a very nice day. Mama and I were to have gone to Worcester to lunch at and see Mr. Wood, but were prevented from going by Mama's having a very bad stiff neck, so she does not move out of her sitting room. We did not go out in the morning but Louisa Herbert and I did and had a nice walk round the park. We were very cosy us three being together; we could talk of things that interest us, not but that I like walking with Mama very much, but when Papa and Mama get together, they talk of their own concerns which do not interest us much.

Tuesday, 19th November. Today we kept Louisa's birthday, and so of course had a holiday. We went out about half past 12. Mama's neck is still very bad, but I think it is better. It is much worse than a common stiff neck; it is much more like the Rheumatics.

Wednesday, 20th November. Mama's neck is still very bad, but she managed to go out for a little while in the afternoon. It was much finer today than it has been lately. At last we have got a place made for our Bantams, but it has been painted so they cannot go in it yet. She laid two eggs in a tree, which fell down and broke.

Thursday, 21st November. A nice frosty day. In the morning we took a nice long walk to the Bishop's wood. Louisa, Herbert and I, as Mama says we may go out now without Burgess. In the afternoon Papa Mama and I went a little in the garden and then went round the park. The Bantams laid another egg last night. Since last Sunday, Louisa has been "out", she was 17 on that day (being her birthday). Mama says she does not know to dress her, for the Stourport and Worcester Ball, which I believe will take place in January.

Friday, 22nd November. A very disagreeable foggy day, but the thermometer was at 32 last night which is frost.

Saturday, 23rd November. Very disagreeable day in the morning so we did not go out but the afternoon being much finer we went out and did the garden. I have just been very ill-natured to Herbert in not picking up something of his that he asked me to do.

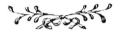

Sunday, 24th November. Very fine in the afternoon but not in the morning.

Monday, 25th November. Very fine in the afternoon but not in the morning. In the afternoon Mama and I went to the School, and Louisa and Herbert out riding. Herbert and I draw a little of an evening now, and one day I was very much hurt by Mama's saying to my face, that Herbert drew the best. I am happy to say Mama thinks of asking the Sullivans again at Christmas.

Tuesday, 26th November. Another frost, Thermometer at 27 last night. Took a long walk in the morning and another in the afternoon, so I am rather tired. We had a nice conversation at dinner about the worlds, and whether there were worlds before this, and whether there will be one after this.

Wednesday, 27th November. Another frost, but not quite so hard as the last one. In the afternoon we went to Norchard to see a Mrs. Wilks. It is about 5 miles there and back, so that I am rather tired today too. I was much pleased at luncheon to hear Mama say that I was grown very good, and Papa said that always made people healthy and that that was the reason I had grown so healthy; that is, much more than I used to be, because now I generally take a dose once a month, and am by no means healthy, not so much as I used to be when I was quite a little child.

Thursday, 28th November. Took another very long and exploring walk, so that I am very tired indeed just now. In the morning, Mama and I went to Witley to call upon Charles and Minnie Stuart who are staying there for a few days on their way to York as he has lately been made Brigade Major. We heard today that Henry Sullivan has got an appointment to the Navy, but there is some objection to his only being able to see with one eye. He will be very sorry if he cannot go, but I believe Uncle John is come to town to see about it.

Friday, 29th November. A very nasty day indeed, did not go out in the morning, but did for a little while in the afternoon, but it rained a little all the time, so it was very disagreeable. I believe Mama has asked the Yorkes to come here on the 9th Dec., to stay till the 13th Dec.

Saturday, 30th November. A very nasty day indeed; did not go out in the morning, but in the afternoon Mama and I went out to call upon Mrs. Lea, and D. Lady Winnington. Mama had an invitation today for a dance at Mrs. Farley's on the same day as the Stourport Ball, and the question was whether Louisa should go to Stourport or Mrs. Farley's, but I believe it will be Stourport.

December
1844

Sunday, 1st December. A very nasty day but went to Church both morning and afternoon. Had a letter from Henry this morning. I think he will be here on the 18th.

Monday, 2nd December. A very fine frost in the morning, but as usual it clouded over in the afternoon; we took a nice walk in the afternoon; saw the hare and met the harriers. Mama told them which way it had gone, so I hope (as the man knew us) that they will make us a present of it. The man called Mama by her name, so I suppose he knew her.

Tuesday, 3rd December. Another very nasty day. Mama has not been very well today, but I think it is more the bad weather than anything else; walked to Stourport in the afternoon.

Wednesday, 4th December. Actually a fine day. Mama and Papa went to Malvern today to stay till Saturday, which is rather a long time for her to be away, but Papa is going to consecrate a church at Malvern and then they are going to Lady Beauchamp's for one night. Herbert and I have been making a water-fall in the River Hartle (a name we give the stream in the park) and I got my foot in the water so of course I got wet.

Thursday, 5th December. Today Louisa and I wrote to Mama. In the morning we took a walk by the Bishop's wood and met the Baker boys going to Mr. Niven. They were playing with a ball on a high rock. Louisa spoke to them; I mumbled something to them, Herbert did nothing and they nodded.

Friday, 6th December. Wrote to Mama again today, and Louisa heard from her this morning. This morning we took a walk to Jone's wood, and in the afternoon Herbert and I went on with our water-fall in the River Hartle.

Saturday, 7th December. Today Mama and Papa came home at half past one A.M. Took a long walk in the morning, and in the afternoon we went out with Papa and Mama. The Thermometer was at 18 last night, which was very cold for a frost before Christmas. Mama had a letter from Mrs. G. Yorke yesterday saying that, as Joey must be at school at that time, and as he did not sleep at the school, and he could not go to their house by himself, they could not come. Mama had a letter this morning from her, saying that a friend had come to Birmingham who would take him to their house while they come here, but he would not be able to come, so Mama wrote to say that she hoped she would bring Edith.

Sunday, 8th December. Very cold indeed; went to Church morning and afternoon; in the evening Herbert found a little gold pencil-case that he had lost, in poor dear Binny's desk. She had taken care of it for him. All her money and everything was there, but I thought Papa had got them all.

Monday, 9th December. It snowed a little last night, so the ground was just white this morning; did not go out in the morning, but in the afternoon Mama, L. H. and I walked to Peppole to give Mrs. Wilks some flannel for her baby. Papa fell down stairs this morning and hurt his back, but he says it is only a bruise. There was a housemaid came for a place today about as tall as me, so Mama said it was no use having her, as she could not do anything. A very disagreeable cold foggy day, but it did not snow.

Tuesday, 10th December. I had a little sore throat in the morning which got much worse in the afternoon. The Grantham Yorkes came in the afternoon about half past 5, and brought Edith and Alice instead of Joey who they meant to bring. Edith is 10 and Alice 8, but they are very short for their age; had a dinner party in the evening, Mr. Baker, Mrs. Baker, Mr. Mrs. and Miss Syncox Lea, Mr. and Mrs. Hone, Messrs. Niven and Hill dined here. Louisa and I played a Duet and Edith and Alice played a Duet, they played very nicely and always by heart.

Wednesday, 11th December. Did not go out either morning or afternoon as my cold was very bad, but wrote to Mary Drummond in the morning, and in the afternoon Herbert went to the Bakers to slide. I do not think either Edith or Alice are pretty but Alice is much the prettiest, they are very much tanned which I suppose comes from always wearing low frocks; we danced in the evening.

Thursday, 12th December. My cold is still very bad, so I did not go out again either morning or afternoon. I played at Battledore and Shuttlecock with Mr. Yorke and in the afternoon I played at different games with Edith and Alice.

Friday, 13th December. My cold still very bad, I did not get up till after breakfast as Mama thought that it would do me good to lie in bed. The Yorkes went at half past ten; I like Mrs. Yorke very much, but I have no very great affection for the two children Edith and Alice, except that they are very nice *little* girls. Though Edith is 10 years old, she is so short and

[81]

so childish in all her ways, that I cannot make her a friend. Mama went to the Coventry's at half past one and comes home tomorrow. It seems that there is no end to her going out. It snowed a little all day, but I hope they will not get snowed up at the Coventry's.

Saturday, 14th December. Mama came back about 5 P.M., bringing Louisa's dress for Stourport Ball. I did not get up till after breakfast as my cold is still very bad.

Sunday, 15th December. It snowed this morning so none of us went to church and I layed in bed all morning. Mama read prayers in my room, and Herbert read a sermon. I got up after dinner and Mama and Herbert went to church but Louisa and I having colds did not go. The Peels came home yesterday and Augusta is in *long ringlets* instead of having her hair plaited up, as it used to be done. I should not think she looked nice, but I have not seen her yet. I suppose Georgy Baker must have them too now, as she always imitates Augusta Peel in dress. I hope we shall see her soon.

Monday, 16th December. My cold is rather better today, and I got up directly after breakfast. It rained all morning, and was very nasty in the afternoon. Mama dined at the Pakingtons in the evening.

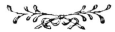

Tuesday, 17th December. Another very nasty day: my cold is much the same as it was yesterday. Mama went to the Peels in the afternoon but they said nothing about the ball on the 1st of January (Augusta's birthday) so I suppose they will not have one, but I hope they will. Mama saw "the *Ringlets*" but it was so dark that she could not see how she looked. Mama dined at the Claughtons this evening.

Wednesday, 18th December. My cold is still uncomfortable but is more in my head, so it is better.

Thursday, 19th December. My cold is rather worse today, so Mama gave me a Dose, which I daresay will do me good. Miss Onerton (the dressmaker) came today to measure me for a new evening frock.

Friday, 20th December. Went to school this morning with Mama to give them the money for the Penny Club. That is the first time I have been out for 11 days. I did not go out in the afternoon. Henry came home from Cambridge about half past 5. He is generally very cross to me, but I think either he or I get better, for he was not so bad last time he was here. He was 20 last birthday. We heard today that *"Miss Carless"*!! was going to be married!!!!!!! to "Mr. Tattersall"!!!!!!!! and to keep a "Carriage and horses"!!!!!! Only fancy!!! I believe she knew his first wife. He lives in Grosvenor Place, up a little dirty court, and no private entrance to his house. Nana heard last night from Mrs. Peel's gardener that Mrs. Peel was going to have a ball!! as she had last year, and that it is going to be either on the 30th or the 31st.

Saturday, 21st December. Today the Sullivans came at about half past 5, Aunt Jane, Emie and Freddy, not Augustus as he is in Wales, which is rather a blessing; they stay till next Saturday. In the afternoon we walked to Stourport.

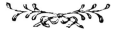

Sunday, 22nd December. Herbert and I did not go to church, as he has got a cold and mine is still too bad though much better. In the afternoon, neither Emie nor Freddy nor Herbert nor me went to church, so we were very merry together. I like Emie better and better; she is so very good-natured.

Monday, 23rd December. A very disagreeable day indeed, so we none of us went out in the morning but in the afternoon Henry and Herbert went out, and Mama and Louisa went to Worcester, and I Emie and Fred-

dy played at different games. Louisa Herbert Emie and I learnt the
Mazurka Waltz.

Tuesday, 24th December. In the morning a Mistletoe was brought in to
the schoolroom and in the afternoon some Holly was brought in which
we made into the words "Jolly Christmas", it was very difficult and we
pricked out fingers a great deal. Herbert nailed it up and Emie and
I shaped and cut it the right lengths: it was my thought and every body
admired it very much. I thought of "Christmas" and Herbert thought of
putting "Jolly" before it. We made a wreath of laurels and put it on old
Homer's head, that is on a bust of him: we had capital fun all the afternoon. We had a very jolly tea and altogether spent a very merry
Christmas Eve. In the evening Papa read Pickwick to the great amusement of the Sullivans, and we set up till half past ten as the servants were
dancing.

Wednesday, 25th December. A very melancholy beginning to
Christmas day, as the *house has been on fire.* About 5 o'clock this
morning I woke and smelt a very strong smell of smoke, and besides I was
so hoarse I could hardly speak. I woke Louisa and she immediately said
"What a very strong smell of smoke there is here", and she got up for the
rush-light which is generally outside the door, but as it happened it was
not there last night, so she knocked at Mama's door and found Papa
getting up for just the same thing. Mama rung the bell for Nana who came
down coughing and with a light, which when she brought into the room,
showed us that the room was so thick with smoke that we could hardly
see even with a candle. I got up to see what was going on, and Mama said
"Go back into your room, this room is so full of smoke", but our room
was much worse. All this time we could hardly speak, as the smoke nearly suffocated us. Then Nana came in and said that she thought the Still-
room fire had just been lit, but it had been put out, and that she thought
the smoke was clearing off. Soon after she came up saying "Oh! dear! my
Lord! Oh dear! Oh dear, what shall we do, the Schoolroom is on fire,
what shall we do!" Upon which Mama told us to put on our Cloaks and

[84]

Bonnets, Stockings and Shoes, in case we should have to go out of doors; Louisa found time to put on her dressing-gown, which I did not, as I was "next door" to being suffocated with smoke. We all went down to the hall "en chemise" with one cloak on. Louisa and I shivered with cold, at 5 o'clock in the morning in a nightgown, in a cold hall on a cold morning. What a nice situation! Papa proposed our going to the Bakers, but we thought it would be rather cold walking up the cold avenue, and that we should be quite safe in the hall, as it was stone; the only chance of its catching was if it should come through the roof which was not likely. We put on some more cloaks and then made ourselves as busy as we could, by taking different things into the great hall; we woke up all the maids and everybody rung the bell at the top of the house, as an alarm bell: sent Charles into the village to bring all the men he could find; sent Joseph to Stourport for a Fire engine, and then to Kidderminster, so we got two, but the Kidderminster one was too large to come through the hall, so they were obliged to bring the water up in buckets to it, but the Stourport one came through the hall and so down to the moat. Fortunately the fire kept in the Schoolroom and so the Engines soon put it out. Papa went into the room soon after it had been put out, and nearly fell into the cellar or under the Schoolroom, as there had been a hole made in the floor, which he did not see, but somebody got him out as he was hanging by his hands. We kept on one of the Engines for some time, as the fire broke out every now and then a little. The whole schoolroom is quite burnt, and everything spoilt that was in it, but some of our things were got out, but they are quite spoilt, partly by the fire, partly by the smoke, and partly by the water from the fire engine. Papa thinks that the fire must have broke out in the drawingroom, but I do not know exactly how. We make the dining room our sitting room, and Louisa and I sleep in the Chintz room, Papa and Mama in the Orange room, Aunt Jane and Emie in the Blue room. Our room I believe has had the boards taken up, and all that side of the house has something the matter with it so we live on the other side. Luckily Papa is insured for a good deal, and there is only the schoolroom that is quite spoilt. Papa is going to send for either Mr. Hayward or Hart to build it up again, I never was in a house on fire before, and hope I never shall be again.

[85]

Thursday, 26th December. In the morning Henry and Herbert went out, but we ladys did not, and in the afternoon Henry read one of Dicken's new books called "The Chimes" but he read so unintelligibly that I shall be obliged to read it again to myself. A great many people have sent to enquire after us, and most of them think that Papa's library has been quite burnt, which is a great mistake. Papa thinks he shall wait till we go to London before he does anything to the schoolroom; the damage is not near so much as we thought it was; only one side of the room being actually burnt, the rest only blistered. I think the water did more harm to all the boxes than the fire. We shall be obliged to have new desks and work-boxes whenever we get settled.

Friday, 27th December. We still live in the dining room but this afternoon our employment was to carry the books back into Mama's sitting room which had been taken out in case they should be burnt. I increased my cold very much by so doing and was sent to bed very early. Mr. Hayward came down this afternoon.

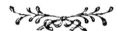

Saturday, 28th December. My cold is dreadfully bad today. I did not get up till after breakfast and then I could hardly see. I could not do anything all day, as my eyes were so dreadfully weak. Mr. Barnett came in the afternoon to see both me and Mama as she has got a very bad cold too. Mr. Barnett thought I might be going to have the measles, and so did Mama, so I went to bed at 5 o'clock, put a mustard poultice on my throat took some horrid powder and was not allowed to talk.

Sunday, 29th December. A great deal better today, but stayed in bed all day. Mr. Barnett came at 10 o'clock A.M. and said he could not see any rash so he did not think I had got the measles, but he said he must keep me in bed all day, and I had to take some horrid mixture every 4 hours. Mama's cold is still very bad indeed. In the afternoon Emie and Louisa got the cat up in my room and *mesmerised* her, that is she went fast asleep and looked very comfortable. Louisa has just been reading "Laing on Mesmerism" so she is full of it. Mama has a great horror of it. She thinks it is either all imposture or else the work of the "Evil Spirit". I hope my cold will be well enough to go to Mrs. Peel's ball on Friday, as I should be very sorry to be disappointed of that. Louisa's ball dress came home yesterday.

Monday, 30th December. Things go on just the same, so there is hardly anything to put down. My cold is much better today, I got up but did not go downstairs. Mama's is still very bad.

Tuesday, 31st December. The Sullivans went away at 11. Poor little Freddy was dreadfully sorry to go, and so was Emie, and I am sure I was very sorry for them to go. We feel very dull now they are gone. Mr. Barnett was in the room to witness our affectionate parting with of course many promises of writing to one another. Elizabeth Whately, the sister of the "Blue Bag" came today to stay for some time, but I do not know how long. My cold is very much better today, and I went downstairs. To-morrow is New Year's day!!! The day Mama gives us our present — Hoorah!

January
1845

Wednesday, 1st January, 1845. Of course I was dressed to breakfast this morning, as that is the time when our presents are given. On going downstairs Herbert and I found *the* box, and on opening it we found the "New fashionable game of 'Cockamaroo'" which I believe is the same as Chinese Billiards, and is the game that we always thought it would be. Henry's present was a "Pictorial Edition of Shakespeare" in 8 volumes, and very handsomely bound. Louisa's present was a pretty gold bracelet, set with enamel and pearls, which was very pretty indeed. Besides the glorious presents Papa gave Louisa £2, Herbert £1 and me £1, which he thought would help to pay off Bills. Besides this Mama gave me a shilling which she owed me as she bet I should lose my ring before today, and I have not.

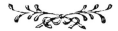

Thursday, 2nd January. Lady Sarah Murray, Miss M. and Mr. M., Mrs. Jenkinson and 2 Miss J's came here today all for the Stourport Ball, which was Louisa's first public ball, and she enjoyed the thoughts of very much, but I have not heard anything about it yet, as she will not be home till about 3 o'clock tomorrow morning, I suppose.

Friday, 3rd January. My cold is getting much better now. Of course people did not get up till about 10 o'clock this morning, as they were so late last night. Louisa enjoyed her ball very much, and was dressed in net over white satin which looked very nice. When they got there they found

Georgy Baker there, who is only 14, but I believe it was all the Peel's doing. We went to a ball at the Peel's tonight, in honour of Augusta's birthday which is on the first. We went at half past 9 and found a great many people there, among others *Miss Percival*, but fortunately for me no Master Percival, as he has actually got a place in the Treasury. Poor Mrs. Peel has got a desperate bad cold, and so has Mr. Peel. I danced nearly every dance, but every one with people I did not know the names of, as I never can hear them when I am introduced to them. Augusta Jenkinson enjoyed herself as much as anybody; she is such a funny girl. We had Lancers, Quadrilles, Polkas, Waltz's Mazurkas and all sorts of dances. The room was very prettily arranged, and altogether it was very nice, though I scarcely knew anybody. They had a beautiful band from Birmingham. I think there were about 110 dancers besides the Chaperons.

Saturday, 4th January. Of course we did not get up till about 10 o'clock, as we did not come home till 4 the night before, but I was not very tired. The Jenkinsons went at 1 and the Murrays at 3, and now we are left alone again, except William Pepys and Elizabeth Whately. Louisa and I moved into our own room tonight for the first time since the fire. Mr. Murray has been sleeping in it lately, but last night he said it was full of smoke, but I hope the fire will not break out again. I liked the ringlets on Augusta much better than I expected. Of course Georgy Baker has got them too now, as she must be like Augusta. We talk of going to London, on the 31st of this month, as Papa has some business to do in town. I like it but Louisa does not much.

Sunday, 5th January. In the morning I went to church for the first time for 4 Sundays, as my cold has been so bad, but in the afternoon I did not go, as my cold is still too bad to come home at 5 o'clock at night, so I wrote to Emie and Herbert wrote to Freddy. It is very warm today indeed and does not feel as if the 8th was to be the coldest day of the season, which is what Murphy foretells.

Monday, 6th January. Another very warm day, and we took a walk in the morning, in the afternoon we took another very long walk, so that I am very tired, as I have not taken a long walk for a very long time. We began our lessons today for the first time since the fire, that is, as many as were not burnt, which most of them were.

Tuesday, 7th January. A very foggy day, so we did not go out in the morning, but in the afternoon Papa, Mama Louisa and Elizabeth went to Stourport and brought home 2 books "Hope on hope ever" for me by Mary Howitt and "The Vicar and the Vicarage" for Herbert. This morning I wrote to Harriet Tyler, as she told me to give her an account of the Peel's ball. Last night we learnt the Waltz a deux temps, the Stalking Step in the Polka and the Mazurka.

Wednesday, 8th January. This is the day that Murphy said would be the coldest day of the season, and it is very cold indeed. In the morning Mama and I went to the school, but in the afternoon we did not go out as it was so bitter cold. (I think I have increased my cold a little from going to the school in the morning.)

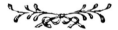

Wednesday, 8th January. Another very cold raw day indeed, so I and Herbert did not go out in the morning or afternoon but we played at Cockamaroo together in the afternoon. Louisa, Mama Papa and Henry, Elizabeth and William dined at Mrs. Peel's tonight and Herbert and I were left alone, and looked at several nice things in the Encyclopoedia, such as *Anatomy, Midwifery* etc. etc. etc. but Mama told me to go to bed 10 minutes before 9 so we had not much time. Herbert and I always go together let one another into all our secrets that we would not tell anybody else for worlds. I had a sort of brow ague last night, it was very painful indeed.

Thursday, 9th January. Another very cold day. In the afternoon the Murrays came to go to the Kidderminster ball with Mama, but as they have not come home yet I cannot give the description of it.

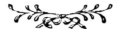

Friday, 10th January. This morning I did not get up till 9 o'clock, as there was no use in getting up before Louisa. The Murrays went at 11 o'clock and in the afternoon Mama and I went to call upon Mrs. Claughton who was not at home, but we found her sister-in-law Mrs. Dudley Ward. I do not think Louisa liked the Kidderminster ball near so well as the others, but I think she enjoyed herself very much. She danced all the Quadrilles, but not the Polkas and Waltz's as Mama does not like us to dance them in company, that is at a public ball. Henry and William (I think I forgot to put that William Pepys came last Thursday week) went to Pull Court today to come back at night, but I think they will hardly have time to come home before dinner. The two Whatelys Henry and Arthur came today to go home tomorrow.

Saturday, 11th January. A much finer day; Elizabeth, Henry and Arthur Whately went about 9 o'clock in the morning; in the afternoon Henry William and Herbert went in the boat, Papa Louisa and I went round the park and Mama went to Ribbesford. Lady Gore and 2 Miss Gores came here this morning to stay till Luncheon, and then went away again.

Sunday, 12th January. A dense fog all day so we did not go to church either morning or afternoon.

Monday, 13th January. It rained hard all morning, so we did not go out, but in the afternoon we went round the park etc. Henry and William rode to the Hundred house today, had luncheon there and then went up Woodbury Hill. I heard from Harriet Tyler today, in return for the letter I wrote to her.

Tuesday, 14th January. This afternoon Mama went away, not to come back till Saturday. Papa, Henry, William and Louisa went too, they are going to Mrs. Jenkinson's for the Worcester Hunt Ball and then go to Lady Emily Foley at Stoke for the Hereford ball, so Louisa has plenty of going out for her first beginning. I heard from Emie this morning; two letters running is something very extraordinary for me. Herbert and I are left alone now, and as he is at Mr. Niven's half the day it is very dull for me. Till Saturday is such a very long time for Mama to be away. We did not go out this morning, as it was a very disagreeable day, but in the afternoon we went out a little while. I like William very much, and am very sorry that he is gone, which he is, from me, as he goes home tomorrow.

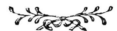

Wednesday, 15th January. This morning we wrote to Mama and then as it poured, we did not go out, nor in the afternoon, as it did the same.

Thursday, 16th January. This morning we played in the River Hartle, which we also did in the afternoon, as it is a nice amusement on a fine day. Herbert and I are very jolly together sometimes, but when he is at Mr. Niven's I am rather dull.

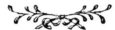

Friday, 17th January. This morning Herbert and I took down barrows full of stones to the River Hartle, with which we paved the sides. We have heard from Mama every day since she has been away, and we have written to her as often; she comes home tomorrow I am happy to say.

Saturday, 18th January. Mama came home about 5, and now I do not think she will leave us again till we come back from London, which is a great blessing. Papa thought yesterday of not going to London till after Easter, as he has some church or other to be consecrated which will interfere, but I think all the same we shall go at the time we always meant to go which is the 31st of this month; we all like it much better. Papa had a letter from Mr. Hayward this morning to say that the Insurance Office would pay 143£ besides the repairing of the room, and Mama means to give us what we want and then give the bill to Papa, which is a very nice arrangement.

Sunday, 19th January. This morning we went to church though it rained, but as Henry has got a swelled heel, from dancing he did not go to church in the afternoon, and I stopped at home to take care of him, that is I did not want to go to church and Mama told me I might stay.

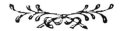

Monday, 20th January. This morning Mama and I went to the school, and in the afternoon took a walk. It is at last settled that we go to London on the 31st, which I am very glad of. It is not yet settled whether we go to Birmingham with 4 horses or 2. Lady Taylor and Chaddy came today to stay till Saturday. Mama had an invitation from Lady M. Cocks today to go on Tuesday and stay till Wednesday, so that is not a very long time.

Tuesday, 21st January. All today Mama and I have been busy in the garden, having another walk made up in the bank. Chaddy has got the Rheumatics in her leg, and it was a great doubt whether she would be able to come here or not, but she is better today. She is not near so pretty as she used to be, but she is a very nice girl; she is just 20, so I suppose she will soon be married, as every body likes her very much.

Wednesday, 22nd January. This morning, as it was a very disgusting day, we did not go out, but in the afternoon we took a walk, and to our great surprise, a little while after we had come in, Herbert went out of the room for something, and he came back, bringing Master Joey Yorke, who is the son of Grantham Yorke, and is about Herbert's age. He and Mr. Yorke came over from Birmingham, he to ask Papa some questions or other, and he brought Joey to see us. He is a very nice boy indeed, and though we have not seen [him] since we were at Westmill, and when I left there I was only 6 or 7 years old, in about half an hour's time, it seemed as if he had been in the house for weeks. We had not seen him for about 7 years I think, as they left Aspeden before we left Westmill; they went away at 7 so they did not pay a very long visit. Joey is not near so tall as Herbert, but rather good looking than otherwise. We wanted them to sleep here, but they said Mrs. Yorke would be in such a fright if they did not go home.

Thursday, 23rd January. This morning we did not go out as it poured down with rain, but in the afternoon, we took a walk round the park, though it rained all the time. Chaddy's Rheumatism is much better now, but she was not able to dance last night. Next Friday week we go to *London!* I do long for it so. The present arrangement is that I should go on the box with Henry, and Herbert, Mama, Papa and Louisa inside, and Nana and James on the [. . .]   We go with *4 horses* as far as Birmingham. This evening Mr. and Mrs. Claughton, Lady Ward, Messrs. Niven and Southell dined here, and most of them went to see *the burnt room.* Captain Southell is a Roman Catholic, and when he was asked to here on Friday, he said he could not because it was *Fish day.*

Friday, 24th January. This morning some evergreens came for Mama to put in her garden and we had great fun out. There was a very cold North West wind, but Herbert and I got ourselves warm running about, and in the afternoon being much finer, we walked to the saw-mills, but as they were not working we did not see them. This evening Mr. Mrs. and Miss Peel, Messrs. Digby and Ingram and Captain Winnington dined here; Sir Offley Wakeham, Mr. and Mrs. Pakington slept here for one night. Robert and Miss Baker came in the evening and after dinner we danced. The first was a Quadrille, which I danced with Robert Baker, who I think is a little improved in his manner, the next was a Polka, which I danced first with Henry and then with Augusta, who seemed to dance it very nicely, and it was very goodnatured of her to dance it with me, as now she is out I have no right to expect it. The next was the Lancers, which I danced with Herbert as I had no one else to dance with. We went on dancing till 12 when we went to bed pretty well tired.

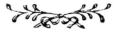

Saturday, 25th January. A nice day, walked to Stourport in the afternoon, and got 2 books to read in the railroad on Friday.

Sunday, 26th January. Today an invitation came from the Queen Dowager to dine at Witley Court on Wednesday the 29th, so we shall not have a great deal of time for packing etc. etc. as tomorrow they dine at Lady Winnington's, Tuesday they dine and sleep at Lady Margaret Cock's, Wednesday they go on to Witley and dine and sleep there, so that they do not come home till Thursday and on Friday we go to *London.* It is the first time they have been asked to sleep at Witley. Not a very fine day, but we went to church both morning and afternoon. In the latter Mama went fast asleep, with her mouth wide open, and her head back. I do not wonder, as we had a very dull sermon indeed from Mr. Niven. Louisa did not go to church in the afternoon as she has got a bad cold: she had a letter this morning from Harriet Tyler, a very long one as hers always are. She asks us to write to her again when we go to London, or rather when we are there. I must answer the one she wrote to me soon.

The End